SAMSUNG GALAXY A16 5G
USER GUIDE FOR SENIORS

The Complete Manual to Master Every
Feature with Confidence and Clarity

MURRAY STRICKLAND

COPYRIGHT © 2025 BY MURRAY STRICKLAND. ALL RIGHTS RESERVED.

No part of this book may be reproduced, duplicated, or transmitted in any form or by any means, including photocopying, recording, or other electronic or mechanical methods, without prior written permission from the author or publisher, except in the case of brief quotations embodied in critical reviews and certain other non-commercial uses permitted by copyright law.

DISCLAIMER

This guide is created for educational purposes and is not officially endorsed by Samsung Electronics. While every effort has been made to ensure accuracy, software features and interface elements may change with updates. Always refer to official Samsung documentation and your Galaxy A16 5G user manual for the most current information. The author assumes no responsibility for any device damage, data loss, warranty issues, or functionality problems resulting from the use of this guide. Always follow proper device care guidelines and Samsung's manufacturer recommendations. Software updates may alter menu locations and feature availability described in this guide.

TABLE OF CONTENTS

INTRODUCTION **8**

Chapter 1: Unboxing and First Impressions **11**

What's Actually in the Box (And What Samsung Didn't Include) 12

Physical Design and Build Quality: The Real Story 13

Initial Setup That Actually Makes Sense 15

Essential Settings You Should Change Immediately 16

First 24 Hours: What to Expect and Avoid 18

Chapter 2: Mastering the Hardware and Controls **20**

Button Layout and Hidden Functions You Didn't Know About 21

Understanding Your Display: Beyond Marketing Specs ... 22

Camera Hardware: What Each Lens Actually Does 24

Ports, Slots, and Connectivity Options Explained 26

Biometric Security: Face vs Fingerprint Reality Check 27

Chapter 3: Android Interface and Navigation Mastery .. **30**

Home Screen Customization That Actually Improves Productivity 31

Navigation Methods: Gestures vs Buttons (Which is Better?) 32

Notification Management Without the Overwhelm 34

Edge Panels and Samsung's Unique Interface Elements .. 36

Multi-Window and Productivity Features That Work 37

Chapter 4: Camera Excellence: Beyond Auto Mode 40

Understanding Each Camera Mode and When to Use Them 41

Manual Controls That Actually Make a Difference 43

Portrait Mode Secrets for Professional-Looking Photos .. 45

Video Recording Tips for Content Creators 47

Gallery Organization and Photo Editing Essentials 49

Chapter 5: Connectivity and Communication Mastery .. 53

Wi-Fi, Bluetooth, and Network Optimization 54

Phone Calls and Messaging: Advanced Features Unlocked 56

NFC and Samsung Pay: Real-World Usage Scenarios 58

Hotspot and Tethering: Making Your Phone a Router 60

Emergency Features That Could Save Your Life 62

Chapter 6: Apps, Performance, and Storage Management 66

Pre-installed Apps: Keep, Disable, or Uninstall Guide 67

Performance Optimization for Smooth Daily Use............... 69

Storage Management Strategies That Actually Work........ 71

Battery Life: Real-World Tips for All-Day Usage................. 73

Security and Privacy Settings You Can't Ignore................... 76

Chapter 7: Samsung Ecosystem Integration......................79

Samsung Account: Worth It or Marketing Hype? 79

Galaxy Store vs Google Play: Which Apps to Get Where .. 81

Samsung Health, Notes, and Productivity Apps Deep Dive
.... 83

Smart Switch and Data Migration Done Right...................... 85

Samsung Cloud vs Google Drive: Storage Strategy............. 87

Chapter 8: Advanced Features and Hidden Gems 90

Developer Options and Power User Tweaks 91

Useful Developer Options for seniors:................................ 91

Accessibility Features That Benefit Everyone...................... 92

Automation with Modes and Routines................................... 94

Screen Recording, Screenshots, and Sharing Mastery 96

Gaming Performance and Game Booster Reality................ 98

Chapter 9: Troubleshooting and Maintenance............... 101

Common Problems and Realistic Solutions 102

Phone feels slow or unresponsive:................................... 102

Apps crashing or not opening:	102
Wi-Fi connection problems:	103
Battery draining too quickly:	103
Bluetooth connection issues:	104
Overheating problems:	104
Storage full warnings:	105
When to Restart, Reset, or Seek Professional Help	105
Professional help indicators:	106
Battery Health and Charging Best Practices	107
Charging best practices:	107
Software Updates: Timing and What to Expect	109
Update types:	109
Hardware Care and Longevity Tips	111
Chapter 10: Customization and Personalization	**114**
Themes, Wallpapers, and Visual Customization	115
Sound Profiles and Audio Enhancement	116
Keyboard Customization and Input Methods	118
Lock Screen and Security Customization	120
Making Your A16 5G Truly Yours	122
Chapter 11: Future-Proofing and Long-Term Ownership	**125**

Software Support Timeline and Update Strategy 125

Accessory Ecosystem: What's Worth Buying 127

    Essential accessories: 127

When to Upgrade vs When to Stick with Your A16 5G .. 128

Resale Value Protection and Device Care 130

Preparing for Your Next Samsung Galaxy Device 131

CONCLUSION **134**

INTRODUCTION

Welcome to the most honest and practical guide you'll find for the Samsung Galaxy A16 5G. If you've just unboxed this device or you're considering purchasing one, you've probably noticed something interesting about most user guides – they either read like technical manuals written by engineers for engineers, or they're filled with marketing fluff that tells you how "amazing" every single feature is without actually explaining how to use them effectively. This book is different.

I've spent months with the Galaxy A16 5G as my daily driver, testing every feature in real-world scenarios, dealing with its quirks, and discovering both its genuine strengths and its honest limitations. What you'll find in these pages isn't just a regurgitation of Samsung's official specifications or a sales pitch disguised as guidance. Instead, you'll get the unvarnished truth about what this phone can and cannot do, told in plain English that actually makes sense.

The Galaxy A16 5G sits in an interesting position in Samsung's lineup. It's not trying to compete with flagship phones that cost three times as much, nor is it a bare-bones budget device that cuts corners everywhere. It's Samsung's attempt to deliver a well-rounded smartphone experience at a reasonable price point, and in many ways, they've succeeded.

But like every device, it has its sweet spots and its compromises, and understanding these will transform how you use your phone.

Throughout these pages, you'll find real-world examples, practical tips, and honest advice about what works well and what doesn't. I'll tell you when a feature is genuinely useful and when it's more marketing hype than practical benefit. You'll learn not just how to change settings, but why you might want to change them and what difference it actually makes in daily use. Whether you're switching from an iPhone, upgrading from an older Android device, or this is your first smartphone, this guide will help you make the most of your investment.

This isn't just about learning where buttons are located or how to navigate menus – though we'll cover that thoroughly. It's about understanding how to configure your A16 5G to work the way you actually live and work. You'll discover hidden features that Samsung barely mentions, learn which pre-installed apps are worth keeping and which ones just clutter your experience, and master techniques that will make your phone feel faster, last longer, and serve you better in the long run.

By the time you finish this guide, you won't just know how to use your Galaxy A16 5G – you'll understand it. You'll be confident in customizing it to match your needs, troubleshooting problems when they arise, and getting genuine value from features you might have otherwise overlooked. Most importantly, you'll have realistic expectations about what this device can deliver, which is the foundation of a satisfying long-term relationship with any smartphone.

Let's begin this journey together, and transform your Galaxy A16 5G from just another gadget into a tool that genuinely enhances your daily life.

CHAPTER 1: UNBOXING AND FIRST IMPRESSIONS

There's something uniquely exciting about opening a new smartphone box, especially when you're a senior exploring the latest technology. The Samsung Galaxy A16 5G represents Samsung's thoughtful approach to creating a device that balances modern features with practical usability. As someone who has helped countless seniors transition to smartphones over the years, I can tell you that your choice of the A16 5G shows wisdom – it's powerful enough to handle everything you'll need without the overwhelming complexity of flagship phones that cost twice as much.

What makes this unboxing experience different from other smartphones is Samsung's understanding that not everyone wants to fidget with tiny accessories or decipher cryptic quick-start guides written in microscopic text. The A16 5G packaging reflects a more mature approach to smartphone design, though as you'll discover, Samsung has made some decisions about what to include (and what not to include) that might surprise you. Let's walk through this journey together, from that first moment you lift the lid to those crucial first days of ownership that will set the tone for your entire smartphone experience.

What's Actually in the Box (And What Samsung Didn't Include)

When you first open your Galaxy A16 5G box, you'll find a surprisingly minimal collection of items. This isn't Samsung being cheap – it's actually an environmental decision that affects most smartphone manufacturers today. Here's exactly what you'll discover inside that sleek black box.

The phone itself sits prominently in the center, wrapped in a protective plastic film that you'll want to peel off carefully. Underneath, you'll find a USB-C cable that's about three feet long – perfectly adequate for most charging situations. There's also a SIM ejection tool, which looks like a tiny metal pin, and some paperwork including a quick start guide and warranty information.

Now, here's what Samsung didn't include that might catch you off guard: there's no wall charger in the box. This means you'll need to use a USB wall adapter you already own, or purchase one separately. Any USB charger that puts out at least 15 watts will work fine, though Samsung sells a 25-watt fast charger that's worth considering. You also won't find earbuds or headphones, which were once standard inclusions.

The absence of a screen protector might concern you, but honestly, the A16 5G's screen is quite durable for normal use.

However, if you're prone to dropping things or want extra peace of mind, consider purchasing a tempered glass screen protector and a basic case. These additions will cost about $20-30 total but can save you hundreds in repair costs.

One pleasant surprise is the quality of the included USB-C cable. Unlike some manufacturers who include flimsy cables that break after a few months, Samsung's cable feels substantial and should last years with normal use. The cable supports fast charging, so when you do get a proper charger, you'll be able to take advantage of the phone's quick charging capabilities.

Physical Design and Build Quality: The Real Story

Holding the Galaxy A16 5G for the first time, you'll immediately notice it feels more substantial than you might expect from a mid-range phone. At 7.9mm thick and weighing 200 grams, it strikes a nice balance – substantial enough to feel quality-built, but not so heavy that it becomes uncomfortable during extended use. For seniors who might have arthritis or grip concerns, this weight distribution actually helps with handling security.

The back of the phone features what Samsung calls a "premium plastic" finish, which sounds like marketing speak but actually works quite well in practice. Unlike glass backs that show every fingerprint and feel slippery, this textured plastic provides a secure grip and resists smudges remarkably well. The Dark Blue color option (there's also Light Green and Gold) has a sophisticated look that doesn't scream "budget phone."

The camera bump on the back is noticeable but not excessive. It houses three camera lenses arranged vertically, along with an LED flash. When you place the phone on a flat surface, it will rock slightly due to this bump, but it's not nearly as pronounced as on many other phones. A case will eliminate this entirely if it bothers you.

Button placement shows thoughtful design consideration for daily use. The volume rocker and power button sit on the right side at a height that's comfortable for most hand sizes. The power button doubles as a fingerprint sensor, which works surprisingly well once you get used to it. On the left side, you'll find the SIM card tray, while the bottom houses the USB-C port, speaker, and headphone jack – yes, Samsung kept the headphone jack, which is increasingly rare and genuinely useful.

The 6.7-inch display dominates the front, with slim bezels that give it a modern appearance. There's a small teardrop notch at the top for the front camera, which is far less intrusive than the large notches on some phones. The screen feels smooth to the touch and responds well to both light touches and more deliberate presses, accommodating different touching styles comfortably.

Initial Setup That Actually Makes Sense

The initial setup process for the Galaxy A16 5G has been designed with user-friendliness in mind, though there are still several steps where making the right choice early can save you headaches later. When you first power on your phone by holding the side button for three seconds, you'll be greeted by a welcome screen that starts the setup wizard.

The first important decision is language selection. Take your time here – while you can change this later, it's easier to get it right from the start. The phone will then check for a SIM card. If you're transferring your number from an old phone, make sure your new SIM card is properly inserted before continuing. The SIM tray requires a gentle but firm push with the included tool.

Wi-Fi connection comes next, and this is crucial for downloading updates and restoring data. Choose your home network carefully and make sure you enter the password correctly. The phone will test the connection and may immediately start downloading a system update, which is actually a good thing – let it finish before proceeding.

Google account setup is where many seniors get confused, but it's simpler than it appears. If you already have a Gmail account or use YouTube, you have a Google account. Enter those same credentials here. If you don't have one, you can create it during setup, but consider asking a tech-savvy family member to help you choose a username you'll remember.

The phone will ask about restoring data from another device. If you're coming from another Android phone, Samsung's Smart Switch feature works remarkably well for transferring contacts, photos, and even some app data. For iPhone users, the process is more limited but still helpful for contacts and photos. Don't worry if you skip this step – you can always transfer data manually later.

Essential Settings You Should Change Immediately

Once you've completed the basic setup, there are several settings you should adjust right away to optimize your Galaxy A16 5G experience. These changes will make your phone more accessible, secure, and pleasant to use on a daily basis.

Start with the display settings by going to Settings > Display. Increase the font size to "Large" or even "Huge" if you need it – there's no shame in making text easier to read. The screen zoom setting can also be adjusted to make icons and interface elements larger. Under the same menu, set your screen timeout to at least 2 minutes so the display doesn't turn off while you're reading.

Security settings deserve immediate attention. Navigate to Settings > Security and Privacy > Biometrics. Set up the fingerprint scanner on the side button – it's convenient and more reliable than face recognition. Add your index finger from your dominant hand first, then consider adding your thumb as a backup. The setup process will ask you to tap the sensor multiple times from different angles to capture a complete fingerprint map.

Sound and vibration settings can significantly improve your experience. Go to Settings > Sounds and Vibration and adjust the ringtone volume to a comfortable level. More importantly, turn on "Vibrate while ringing" so you'll feel calls even if you don't hear them immediately. Consider setting different ringtones for calls and text messages to distinguish between them audibly.

Accessibility features, found under Settings > Accessibility, offer valuable improvements even if you don't consider yourself to have accessibility needs. "Magnification" allows you to triple-tap the screen to zoom in on any content. "High contrast text" makes words stand out better against backgrounds. "Remove animations" can make the interface feel more responsive by eliminating unnecessary visual effects.

Finally, visit Settings > Apps and look for any apps you definitely won't use. Some pre-installed apps can be disabled (not deleted, but hidden and prevented from running) to reduce clutter. Don't disable anything you're uncertain about – you can always re-enable apps later if needed.

First 24 Hours: What to Expect and Avoid

Your first day with the Galaxy A16 5G should be about getting comfortable with basic functions rather than trying to master every feature immediately. The most important thing to understand is that modern smartphones have a "learning period" where the device adapts to your usage patterns, so performance and battery life will improve over the first few days.

Expect the battery to drain faster than normal during your first day. This happens because the phone is downloading app updates, syncing data, and indexing content in the background. Don't panic if you need to charge it twice on the first day – this is completely normal. By day three or four, you should see much more reasonable battery performance.

Focus on mastering the basic functions first: making calls, sending text messages, and taking a few photos. The Phone app works exactly like you'd expect – tap the green phone icon, enter a number using the on-screen keypad, and tap the green call button. For text messages, use the Messages app with the speech bubble icon. The camera opens by tapping the camera icon or double-pressing the side button quickly.

CHAPTER 2: MASTERING THE HARDWARE AND CONTROLS

Learning your way around a new smartphone can feel like trying to navigate a car where someone has moved all the familiar controls. The Galaxy A16 5G might look similar to other phones you've seen, but Samsung has implemented some thoughtful design choices that make daily use more comfortable for seniors. Understanding these physical elements isn't just about knowing where buttons are located – it's about developing the confidence to use your phone naturally and efficiently.

The beauty of the A16 5G's design lies in its practical approach to hardware. Samsung didn't try to reinvent the wheel with exotic button placements or confusing gestures. Instead, they've refined the basics while adding some genuinely useful features that you might not discover on your own. From hidden shortcuts that can save you multiple taps to display technologies that reduce eye strain, this chapter will help you master the physical aspects of your phone so you can focus on enjoying its capabilities rather than fighting with its controls.

Button Layout and Hidden Functions You Didn't Know About

The Galaxy A16 5G keeps things refreshingly simple with its button arrangement, but there's more functionality packed into these physical controls than meets the eye. On the right side of your phone, you'll find two essential buttons that will quickly become second nature once you understand their full capabilities.

The power button, located about halfway down the right edge, does much more than just turn your screen on and off. A single press wakes the screen or puts it to sleep. However, if you press and hold this button for about three seconds, you'll access the power menu, which gives you options to power off, restart, or enter emergency mode. Here's where it gets interesting: you can customize what happens when you double-press this button. By default, it opens the camera, which is genuinely useful for capturing quick moments. To change this, go to Settings > Advanced Features > Side Button and choose from options like opening your flashlight, voice recorder, or any app you use frequently.

The volume buttons sit just above the power button and have their own hidden talents. Obviously, they control volume during calls, media playback, and ringtones. But during a phone call, if you press the volume up button, it will also turn on the speakerphone – a handy shortcut when your hands are full. When taking photos, either volume button can serve as a shutter button, which is much more natural than trying to tap a small on-screen button.

Here's a particularly useful combination: pressing the power button and volume down simultaneously takes a screenshot. You'll hear a brief camera sound and see a quick animation showing the screen capture. This works from any screen, making it perfect for saving important information, funny messages, or directions.

The left side of the phone houses the SIM card tray, which requires the included ejection tool to open. This isn't something you'll use often, but it's worth noting that the tray can hold either two SIM cards (useful if you travel internationally) or one SIM card plus a microSD card for additional storage.

Understanding Your Display: Beyond Marketing Specs

Samsung markets the A16 5G's display with impressive-sounding specifications, but what really matters is how this screen performs in your daily life. The 6.7-inch display uses what Samsung calls a "Super AMOLED" panel, which delivers notably better contrast and color reproduction than the LCD screens found in many budget phones.

The most practical advantage of this display technology is its excellent visibility in various lighting conditions. Unlike older phone screens that become nearly impossible to read in bright sunlight, the A16 5G automatically adjusts its brightness and contrast to maintain readability outdoors. The screen can reach 800 nits of brightness, which translates to clear visibility even on sunny days when you're checking directions or reading messages.

Color accuracy on this display is genuinely impressive for a mid-range phone. Photos appear vibrant without being oversaturated, and text remains crisp and easy to read. The screen supports a refresh rate of up to 90Hz, which means scrolling through web pages, social media feeds, or your photo gallery feels noticeably smoother than older phones. This isn't just marketing fluff – the difference is immediately apparent and makes the phone feel more responsive to your touch.

The display also incorporates blue light reduction technology, which becomes increasingly important for comfortable extended use. You can access this feature by going to Settings > Display > Eye Comfort Shield. When enabled, it reduces the blue light emission that can cause eye strain, particularly during evening use. The effect is subtle but meaningful for longer reading sessions.

Touch sensitivity has been optimized for users who might not have the firmest grip or steadiest hands. The screen responds well to light touches while still being resistant to accidental activation when the phone is in your pocket or purse. If you're wearing gloves, you can increase touch sensitivity in Settings > Display > Touch Sensitivity.

Camera Hardware: What Each Lens Actually Does

The Galaxy A16 5G sports a triple-camera system on the back, and unlike some phones that include cameras just to boost the count, each lens here serves a genuine purpose. Understanding what each camera does will help you choose the right tool for different photographic situations.

The main camera features a 50-megapixel sensor that handles the majority of your photography needs. This is your go-to camera for everyday photos, offering excellent detail and color reproduction in good lighting conditions. The large sensor size means it gathers more light than typical budget phone cameras, resulting in clearer photos in moderately dim conditions. When you open the camera app, this is the lens that's active by default.

The 5-megapixel ultrawide camera expands your creative possibilities significantly. By tapping the "0.5x" button in the camera app, you switch to this lens, which captures a much wider field of view. This is invaluable for photographing large groups of people, capturing entire buildings without stepping back, or taking landscape photos that include more of the scenery. The image quality isn't quite as sharp as the main camera, but the perspective it provides often makes up for this limitation.

The 2-megapixel macro camera enables close-up photography of small subjects. While Samsung markets this heavily, the practical reality is more limited. The macro camera works best for photographing flowers, insects, or detailed textures when you can get very close to your subject. However, the image quality is modest, and you'll often get better results using the main camera and simply moving closer to your subject.

The front-facing camera, housed in that small notch at the top of the screen, uses a 13-megapixel sensor that's quite capable for video calls and selfies. It includes basic beauty filters that can smooth skin tones, though these effects can look artificial if overused. For video calls on platforms like FaceTime, WhatsApp, or Zoom, this camera provides clear, well-lit images in most indoor conditions.

Ports, Slots, and Connectivity Options Explained

One of the Galaxy A16 5G's most user-friendly features is its comprehensive selection of physical connections, which sets it apart from many modern smartphones that have eliminated useful ports in favor of wireless-only solutions.

The USB-C port on the bottom of the phone serves multiple purposes beyond just charging. This reversible connector means you can't insert the cable upside down, eliminating the frustration of fumbling with cable orientation. The port supports fast charging up to 25 watts when paired with an appropriate charger, which can take your battery from empty to about 50% in roughly 30 minutes. You can also use this port to connect the phone to a computer for transferring files or to external displays using a USB-C to HDMI adapter.

Perhaps most notably, Samsung retained the 3.5mm headphone jack, positioned next to the USB-C port. This might seem old-fashioned, but it's genuinely practical for seniors who already own comfortable wired headphones or prefer the reliability of a physical connection. The audio quality through this jack is excellent, and you'll never have to worry about battery levels in your headphones or connection dropouts that can plague wireless audio.

The speaker system includes a main speaker at the bottom of the phone and uses the earpiece at the top as a secondary speaker for stereo sound during media playback. While not as impressive as flagship phone speakers, the audio quality is clear and loud enough for speakerphone calls or watching videos in a quiet room.

Wireless connectivity options are comprehensive and future-ready. The phone supports Wi-Fi 5 (802.11ac), which provides fast internet connectivity on modern home networks. Bluetooth 5.3 ensures reliable connections to wireless headphones, speakers, and car audio systems with improved range and battery efficiency compared to older Bluetooth versions. NFC capability enables tap-to-pay functionality through Samsung Pay or Google Pay, though this feature requires setup through your banking apps.

Biometric Security: Face vs Fingerprint Reality Check

The Galaxy A16 5G offers two biometric security options, and understanding their practical differences will help you choose the most convenient and secure method for your lifestyle. Both face recognition and fingerprint scanning aim to replace traditional PIN or password entry, but they each have distinct advantages and limitations.

Fingerprint recognition, integrated into the side-mounted power button, represents the more reliable and secure option. The sensor reads the unique patterns of your fingerprint ridges and works consistently regardless of lighting conditions, whether you're wearing glasses, or how you're positioned relative to the phone. Setup involves pressing your finger on the sensor multiple times from slightly different angles, allowing the system to capture a comprehensive fingerprint map.

In daily use, fingerprint unlock works remarkably well. The sensor responds quickly – typically unlocking your phone in less than half a second once you develop the muscle memory to place your finger correctly. You can register up to four different fingerprints, which is useful for adding both thumbs and index fingers to accommodate different holding positions. The fingerprint data is stored locally on your phone and encrypted, making it quite secure against remote hacking attempts.

Face recognition offers convenience but comes with important caveats. The front-facing camera analyzes your facial features to create a digital map for comparison during unlock attempts. Setup is straightforward – you simply hold the phone at arm's length and follow the on-screen prompts to capture your face from different angles. However, this system uses only the standard camera, not specialized infrared sensors like premium phones, which creates some limitations.

In practical use, face unlock works well in good lighting conditions when you're looking directly at the phone. However, it struggles in dim environments, can be fooled by photos in some cases, and won't work if you're wearing sunglasses or a face mask. These limitations make it less reliable than fingerprint scanning for everyday security. For seniors who might have shaky hands or difficulty positioning their finger precisely on the small sensor, face recognition can be more forgiving, but the security trade-offs are worth considering.

The most practical approach for many users is to enable both methods, using face recognition for quick access in ideal conditions and relying on fingerprint scanning when face recognition fails or when enhanced security is needed.

CHAPTER 3: ANDROID INTERFACE AND NAVIGATION MASTERY

Navigating a smartphone interface can feel overwhelming when you're transitioning from a traditional phone or even an older smartphone. The Galaxy A16 5G runs Samsung's One UI Interface on top of Android, which means you're getting two layers of design philosophy working together. The good news is that Samsung has spent considerable effort making their interface more intuitive for users who value clarity over flashiness. Unlike some Android phones that can feel chaotic or overly complex, the A16 5G presents a clean, organized approach to smartphone navigation.

What sets Samsung's approach apart is their understanding that not everyone wants to spend hours customizing every aspect of their phone. The default setup is genuinely usable right out of the box, but there are specific modifications that can dramatically improve your daily experience. This chapter focuses on practical changes that solve real problems rather than cosmetic tweaks that look impressive but don't add value. You'll learn to distinguish between useful customization options and unnecessary complexity, ensuring your phone works for you rather than against you.

Home Screen Customization That Actually Improves Productivity

The home screen serves as your phone's command center, and thoughtful organization here saves countless taps and reduces frustration throughout your day. The Galaxy A16 5G comes with a reasonable default layout, but several strategic changes can transform it into a truly efficient workspace.

Start by evaluating the apps currently on your home screen. Samsung pre-installs numerous apps, many of which you'll never use. Long-press any app icon you don't recognize or need, then drag it to the "Remove" option that appears at the top of the screen. This doesn't delete the app entirely – it just removes the shortcut from your home screen. Focus on keeping only the apps you use at least weekly in these prime real estate locations.

Create a logical arrangement based on your actual usage patterns. Place your most frequently used apps – likely Phone, Messages, Camera, and perhaps a weather app – in the bottom row where they're easiest to reach with your thumb. This dock area appears on every home screen page, making these apps always accessible. Consider grouping related apps into folders to reduce clutter. For example, create a "Health" folder containing any medical apps, fitness trackers, or medication reminders.

Widget functionality offers genuine productivity benefits when used strategically. Swipe to an empty area of your home screen, long-press, and select "Widgets" to see available options. The Weather widget provides at-a-glance conditions without opening an app. The Clock widget can display multiple time zones if you have family in different locations. Most importantly, the Calendar widget shows upcoming appointments directly on your home screen, eliminating the need to open the calendar app for quick reference.

Adjust the grid size to match your vision and dexterity needs. In Settings > Home Screen, you can choose between 4x5, 4x6, or 5x6 app layouts. The 4x5 option creates larger icons that are easier to see and tap accurately, while 5x6 fits more apps on each screen. There's no right answer – choose based on your comfort level.

Finally, consider enabling "Easy Mode" if the standard interface feels too complex. This creates larger icons, simplified layouts, and reduces visual clutter significantly. You'll find this option in Settings > Display > Easy Mode. It's not just for users with vision problems – many people simply prefer the cleaner, less overwhelming appearance.

Navigation Methods: Gestures vs Buttons (Which is Better?)

Samsung gives you two primary methods for navigating your phone: traditional on-screen buttons or modern gesture controls. Each approach has distinct advantages, and the best choice depends on your comfort level with new technologies and your physical dexterity.

The traditional button navigation displays three icons at the bottom of your screen: a back arrow, home circle, and recent apps square. These buttons work exactly as you'd expect – tap back to return to the previous screen, home to return to your main screen, and recent apps to see what's currently running. This method requires no learning curve if you've used any Android phone before, and the buttons are large enough for easy, accurate tapping.

Button navigation offers several practical advantages for seniors. The visual feedback is immediate and obvious – you can see exactly what each button does before tapping it. There's no risk of accidentally triggering the wrong action through an imprecise gesture. The buttons remain consistently positioned, so muscle memory develops quickly. If you have any hand tremor or arthritis that affects fine motor control, buttons provide a more forgiving target than gesture zones.

Gesture navigation eliminates the bottom button bar, giving you more screen space for content. Instead of tapping buttons, you perform specific swipes: swipe up from the bottom to go home, swipe up and hold to see recent apps, and swipe from either edge to go back. Samsung's implementation is more forgiving than some manufacturers, with wider gesture zones that reduce accidental activation.

The learning curve for gestures is steeper, but the payoff includes a more immersive experience and slightly faster navigation once mastered. However, gestures can be frustrating if you frequently miss the precise swipe zones or accidentally trigger actions while trying to scroll content near screen edges.

To switch between methods, go to Settings > Display > Navigation Bar. Try gesture navigation for a few days, but don't hesitate to switch back to buttons if it feels unnatural. There's no performance advantage to either method – this is purely about personal preference and comfort.

Notification Management Without the Overwhelm

Notifications represent one of the biggest sources of smartphone frustration, but properly configured, they become valuable productivity tools rather than constant interruptions. The key is taking control immediately rather than letting apps dictate when and how they demand your attention.

When you first install apps, they'll request notification permissions. The default approach of allowing all notifications creates chaos within days. Instead, be selective from the start. Essential apps like Phone, Messages, and your calendar should have full notification access. Social media apps, games, and promotional apps should have limited or no notification privileges.

Access notification settings through Settings > Notifications. Here you'll find "App Notifications" which lists every installed app and its current notification status. Scroll through this list and disable notifications for any app that isn't time-sensitive. Shopping apps, for example, rarely need to interrupt your day with sale announcements.

For apps you do want notifications from, customize how they appear. Many apps offer multiple notification types – you might want text message alerts but not promotional messages from your carrier. Tap any app in the notification settings to see its specific options. You can typically choose between different types of alerts within each app.

The "Do Not Disturb" feature provides temporary relief when you need uninterrupted time. Schedule it to activate automatically during sleep hours, or enable it manually during meals, meetings, or focused activities. You can customize which notifications break through Do Not Disturb – typically calls from your contacts list and emergency alerts. Lock screen notifications require special consideration. While convenient for checking messages without unlocking your phone, they can also display private information to anyone who picks up your device. In Settings > Lock Screen > Notifications, you can choose to hide notification content on the lock screen while still showing that notifications are waiting.

Edge Panels and Samsung's Unique Interface Elements

Samsung's Edge Panels represent one of their most distinctive interface features, though their usefulness varies significantly depending on your usage patterns. These sliding panels appear when you swipe from the right edge of your screen, providing quick access to apps, contacts, and tools without leaving your current screen.

The Apps Edge panel serves as a customizable app launcher, holding up to 20 frequently used apps in a compact sidebar. This becomes genuinely useful if you find yourself frequently switching between the same set of apps. To customize it, open the Edge Panel, tap the settings gear, and select which apps to include. Focus on apps you use multiple times daily but don't want cluttering your home screen.

People Edge provides one-touch access to your most important contacts, complete with their preferred communication method. You can assign specific contacts to call, text, or email with a single tap. This feature shines for seniors who regularly communicate with a small group of family members or friends. The setup process walks you through selecting contacts and their preferred communication methods.

Tools Edge offers quick access to useful utilities like a flashlight, timer, compass, and ruler. While these tools are available through other apps, having them instantly accessible can be convenient for quick tasks. The flashlight shortcut alone makes this panel worthwhile for many users. Smart Select allows you to capture and share specific portions of your screen, which is more flexible than traditional screenshots. You can capture rectangular areas, oval selections, or even create animated GIFs from screen content. This feature is particularly useful for sharing specific parts of articles, maps, or social media posts.

To enable Edge Panels, go to Settings > Display > Edge Panels and toggle the feature on. You can customize which panels appear and their order based on your preferences. If you find yourself accidentally triggering Edge Panels when holding your phone, you can adjust the sensitivity or disable the feature entirely.

Multi-Window and Productivity Features That Work

Multi-window functionality on the Galaxy A16 5G goes beyond gimmicky demonstrations to provide genuinely useful productivity benefits, particularly for tasks that benefit from viewing multiple sources of information simultaneously.

Split-screen mode divides your display into two sections, each running a different app. This proves invaluable for tasks like comparing prices between shopping websites, referencing directions while texting your location to someone, or taking notes while watching a video tutorial. To activate split-screen, open your recent apps (swipe up and hold, or tap the recent apps button), then tap the app icon at the top of any app card and select "Open in split screen view."

Not all apps support split-screen mode, but most essential apps do, including Samsung Internet, Messages, Gallery, Calendar, and Notes. The split can be adjusted by dragging the divider line between apps, allowing you to allocate more screen space to whichever app needs it most at the moment.
Pop-up view creates floating windows for specific apps, allowing them to overlay your current screen like windows on a computer. This works particularly well for keeping a calculator accessible while working in other apps, or maintaining a video call window while checking your calendar. Enable pop-up view through the same recent apps menu, selecting "Open in pop-up view" instead of split-screen.
App pairs streamline the process of opening specific app combinations you use regularly. If you frequently use split-screen with your navigation app and music player, for

example, you can save this combination as an app pair that opens both apps in split-screen mode with a single tap. Create app pairs from the split-screen view by tapping the three dots between the apps and selecting "Save app pair."

The practical limitations of multi-window are worth acknowledging. Text becomes smaller and harder to read when split between apps. Some apps pause or limit functionality when not in full-screen mode. Battery consumption increases when running multiple apps simultaneously. However, for specific tasks like research, comparison shopping, or reference work, multi-window capabilities can significantly improve efficiency over constantly switching between full-screen apps.

CHAPTER 4: CAMERA EXCELLENCE: BEYOND AUTO MODE

The camera system on your Galaxy A16 5G represents one of the most significant improvements you'll notice over older smartphones, but like any powerful tool, it delivers the best results when you understand how to use it properly. Many seniors initially feel intimidated by camera apps filled with modes, settings, and options that seem designed for professional photographers. The truth is, while the A16 5G does offer advanced capabilities, the most impactful improvements to your photos come from understanding just a few key concepts and techniques.

What makes modern smartphone photography so compelling is that the phone does most of the technical heavy lifting automatically, leaving you free to focus on composition and timing. However, Samsung has included several camera modes and manual controls that can dramatically improve your photos in specific situations. The key is knowing when to step beyond the automatic mode and which alternative to choose. This chapter will guide you through the practical applications of each camera mode, helping you capture better photos of the moments that matter most to you.

Understanding Each Camera Mode and When to Use Them

The camera app opens to Photo mode by default, which handles the vast majority of your photography needs with excellent automatic settings. This mode analyzes your scene and adjusts exposure, color balance, and focus automatically. For everyday photos of family, pets, food, or scenery in decent lighting, Photo mode delivers consistently good results without any input from you.

Step-by-step to access different modes:

1. Open the Camera app
2. Look at the bottom of the screen for mode labels
3. Swipe left or right to change modes
4. Tap "MORE" to see additional options

Portrait mode creates that professional-looking background blur effect that makes your subject stand out dramatically. This works best when photographing people from about 3-8 feet away. The phone uses both cameras to map depth, then artificially blurs the background while keeping your subject sharp.

When to use Portrait mode:

- Taking photos of people, especially close-ups
- When the background is distracting or cluttered
- For formal occasions like birthdays or holidays
- When you want photos that look more professional

Night mode activates automatically in very low light, but you can also enable it manually for better results in dim conditions. The phone takes multiple exposures and combines them to create brighter, clearer photos than would normally be possible. This process takes 2-3 seconds, so hold the phone steady.

Best situations for Night mode:

- Indoor evening gatherings with limited lighting
- Outdoor photos during twilight hours
- Restaurant meals in dimly lit establishments
- Candle-lit celebrations or intimate settings

Pro mode gives you manual control over focus, exposure, and other technical settings. While intimidating at first, you only need to understand two or three controls to see significant improvements in challenging lighting situations.

Food mode optimizes colors and contrast specifically for photographing meals. It creates a subtle blur around the edges while keeping the center sharp, making your food photos more appetizing for sharing with family or on social media.

Manual Controls That Actually Make a Difference

Pro mode might seem overwhelming with its array of technical controls, but focusing on just three key adjustments will handle most situations where automatic mode struggles.

Accessing Pro mode:

1. Open Camera app
2. Swipe to "MORE"
3. Select "PRO"
4. Look for control icons along the bottom

The exposure compensation control (marked "EV") brightens or darkens your photo without changing other settings. This solves the most common photography problem: photos that are too dark or too bright.

Step-by-step exposure adjustment:

1. Tap the EV icon in Pro mode
2. Drag the slider left to darken the image
3. Drag right to brighten the image
4. Watch the preview change as you adjust
5. Take the photo when it looks right

Focus control lets you choose exactly what should be sharp in your photo. Automatic focus sometimes selects the wrong subject, especially in complex scenes with multiple people or objects at different distances.

Manual focus technique:

1. Tap the "FOCUS" control in Pro mode
2. Drag the slider to adjust focus distance
3. Watch the preview to see which areas become sharp
4. Stop when your intended subject is clearest
5. Take the photo

ISO control adjusts the camera's sensitivity to light. Lower numbers (100-400) work best in bright conditions and produce cleaner images. Higher numbers (800-3200) help in dim lighting but may introduce grain.

Practical ISO guidelines:

- Bright outdoor scenes: ISO 100-200
- Indoor lighting: ISO 400-800
- Dim restaurants: ISO 800-1600
- Very low light: ISO 1600-3200

White balance corrects color casts from different types of lighting. Indoor lights often make photos look yellow or orange, while outdoor shade can appear too blue.

Quick white balance fixes:

- Indoor incandescent lights: Select "Tungsten"
- Fluorescent office lighting: Select "Fluorescent"

- Outdoor shade: Select "Cloudy"
- Mixed lighting: Use "Auto" and adjust if needed

Portrait Mode Secrets for Professional-Looking Photos

Portrait mode on the A16 5G produces remarkably good results when you understand its limitations and work within them. The key to professional-looking portraits lies in positioning, lighting, and understanding what makes the background blur effect work properly.

Optimal distance and positioning:

1. Stand 4-6 feet away from your subject
2. Ensure good lighting on the person's face
3. Position the subject against a background that's at least 6 feet behind them
4. Avoid complex backgrounds with many small details

The background blur (called "bokeh") works best when there's significant distance between your subject and the background. A person standing directly against a wall won't produce good results, but the same person standing 6 feet in front of that wall will create beautiful separation.

Lighting tips for better portraits:

- Face the subject toward a window for natural light

- Avoid direct overhead lighting that creates harsh shadows
- Overcast outdoor conditions provide excellent even lighting
- Use the phone's flash only as a last resort

Portrait mode struggles with certain subjects and situations. Understanding these limitations prevents frustration and helps you choose the regular Photo mode when appropriate.

When Portrait mode doesn't work well:

- Subjects with glasses (may blur the lenses incorrectly)
- People with very curly or fine hair (edge detection problems)
- Multiple people at different distances
- Moving subjects (children or pets)
- Complex backgrounds with many similar colors

Composition techniques for better portraits:

1. Focus on the subject's eyes - they should be the sharpest part
2. Leave some space above the person's head in the frame
3. Try both vertical and horizontal orientations
4. Consider the rule of thirds - place eyes about 1/3 down from the top
5. Take multiple shots with slight variations in pose

The portrait mode also includes beauty filters, but use these sparingly. Heavy filtering creates an artificial appearance that often looks worse than the natural photo. If you use beauty effects, keep them at the lowest setting for subtle improvements.

Video Recording Tips for Content Creators

Video recording on the Galaxy A16 5G produces surprisingly good results for family memories, social media content, or video calls with distant relatives. Understanding a few basic principles will dramatically improve your video quality and make your recordings more enjoyable to watch.

Basic video recording setup:

1. Open Camera app
2. Swipe to "VIDEO" mode
3. Tap the record button (red circle)
4. Tap again to stop recording

Stability represents the most critical factor in professional-looking video. Even slight camera movement becomes magnified and distracting in video footage. The A16 5G includes digital stabilization, but proper holding technique remains essential.

Handheld stability techniques:

- Hold the phone with both hands
- Tuck your elbows against your body for support
- Lean against a wall or solid surface when possible
- Move slowly and deliberately when panning

- Consider purchasing an inexpensive phone tripod for static shots

Audio quality often matters more than video quality for viewer enjoyment. The A16 5G's microphones are quite good, but environmental factors significantly impact audio clarity.

Audio recording tips:

- Record in quiet environments when possible
- Stay within 6 feet of your subject for clear speech
- Avoid windy outdoor locations
- Turn off background music or TV during recording
- Speak clearly and at normal volume

Video composition guidelines:

1. Hold the phone horizontally for traditional viewing
2. Keep important action in the center third of the frame
3. Leave some headroom above people in the shot
4. Avoid zooming during recording (walk closer instead)
5. Keep videos short - 30 seconds to 2 minutes work best for sharing

Lighting affects video even more dramatically than still photos. Poor lighting creates grainy, unclear footage that's difficult to watch.

Lighting best practices:

- Face subjects toward windows or other light sources
- Avoid backlighting (light behind the subject)
- Outdoor overcast conditions provide excellent even lighting
- Indoor recording works best near large windows
- Use the phone's LED light only for very close subjects

The A16 5G offers several video resolution options, but 1080p at 30fps provides the best balance of quality and file size for most users. Higher resolutions create larger files that are harder to share and don't display better on most screens.

Gallery Organization and Photo Editing Essentials

The Gallery app on your A16 5G serves as both a photo viewer and a surprisingly capable editing tool. Proper organization and basic editing skills will help you maintain a manageable photo collection and enhance your best shots.

Gallery app navigation:

1. Open Gallery app from home screen
2. Photos display in chronological order by default
3. Tap "Albums" to see organized collections
4. Use search to find specific photos quickly

Samsung automatically creates several useful albums that help organize your photos without manual sorting:

Automatic album categories:

- Camera: All photos taken with your phone's camera
- Screenshots: Screen captures and saved images
- Videos: All recorded videos in one location
- Favorites: Photos you've marked with the heart icon
- Recently added: Your newest photos and downloads

Creating custom albums helps organize photos by events, people, or subjects. This becomes particularly valuable as your photo collection grows over hundreds or thousands of images.

Creating custom albums:

1. Open Gallery app
2. Tap "Albums" at the bottom
3. Tap the "+" icon to create new album
4. Name your album (Wedding, Vacation, Grandchildren, etc.)
5. Add photos by selecting them and choosing "Move to album"

The built-in photo editor provides essential tools for improving your photos without needing additional apps. These adjustments can transform a mediocre photo into one you're proud to share.

Basic editing steps:

1. Open any photo in Gallery
2. Tap the pencil icon at the bottom
3. Choose from editing options across the bottom
4. Make adjustments using sliders
5. Tap "Save" to preserve changes

Essential editing tools:

- **Brightness**: Lightens or darkens the entire image
- **Contrast**: Makes darks darker and lights lighter for more dramatic photos
- **Saturation**: Increases or decreases color intensity
- **Crop**: Removes unwanted edges or changes photo proportions
- **Rotate**: Fixes photos taken at wrong angles

Practical editing guidelines:

- Make small adjustments rather than dramatic changes
- Edit brightness first, then contrast and saturation
- Crop tightly around your main subject
- Save the original before making major edits
- Don't over-saturate colors - subtle is usually better

The Gallery app also includes automatic enhancement features that can improve photos with minimal effort. The "Auto" button analyzes your photo and applies appropriate adjustments automatically. This works well for about 70% of photos, though you can always undo changes if you don't like the results.

CHAPTER 5: CONNECTIVITY AND COMMUNICATION MASTERY

Staying connected in today's world goes far beyond making simple phone calls. Your Galaxy A16 5G serves as a communication hub that can connect to multiple networks simultaneously, handle various types of messaging, enable contactless payments, and even provide internet access to other devices. For seniors who may remember when a phone call required an operator's assistance, the connectivity options available today can seem overwhelming, but they also offer unprecedented convenience and safety features.

The key to mastering connectivity on your A16 5G lies in understanding which features genuinely improve your daily life versus those that add unnecessary complexity. This chapter focuses on practical applications that solve real communication challenges – from ensuring reliable internet access wherever you are to using emergency features that could prove lifesaving. We'll cut through the technical jargon to focus on what actually works in everyday situations.

Wi-Fi, Bluetooth, and Network Optimization

Your Galaxy A16 5G manages multiple types of wireless connections simultaneously, switching between them intelligently to maintain the best possible internet access and device connectivity.

Setting up Wi-Fi connections:

1. Go to Settings > Connections > Wi-Fi
2. Toggle Wi-Fi on if it's not already active
3. Select your home network from the list
4. Enter your network password carefully
5. Tap "Connect" and wait for confirmation

Once connected, your phone remembers trusted networks and connects automatically when in range. The A16 5G prioritizes Wi-Fi over mobile data to save on cellular usage and often provides faster speeds.

Wi-Fi optimization tips:

- Position yourself closer to your router for stronger signals
- Restart your router monthly by unplugging for 30 seconds
- Use 5GHz networks when available (often labeled with "5G" suffix)
- Forget old networks you no longer use: Settings > Wi-Fi > Saved networks

Bluetooth connects your phone to wireless accessories like headphones, speakers, or car audio systems. Modern Bluetooth is more reliable than older versions, but proper pairing remains important.

Bluetooth pairing process:

1. Put your accessory in pairing mode (check device instructions)
2. Go to Settings > Connections > Bluetooth
3. Ensure Bluetooth is turned on
4. Tap "Scan" to find nearby devices
5. Select your device from the list
6. Follow any on-screen pairing prompts

Common Bluetooth connection issues and solutions:

- **Device won't appear**: Ensure it's in pairing mode and close enough (within 30 feet)
- **Connection drops frequently**: Check for interference from other wireless devices
- **Poor audio quality**: Keep devices within 10 feet and avoid obstacles
- **Won't reconnect automatically**: Delete the pairing and set up again

Mobile network optimization ensures reliable cellular service and efficient data usage. The A16 5G supports 5G networks where available, automatically falling back to 4G LTE when needed.

Network settings optimization:

1. Go to Settings > Connections > Mobile networks
2. Set Network mode to "5G/LTE/3G/2G (auto connect)"
3. Enable "Data roaming" only when traveling internationally
4. Turn on "Smart network switch" for seamless Wi-Fi/mobile transitions

Phone Calls and Messaging: Advanced Features Unlocked

The Phone app includes features that extend far beyond basic calling, offering tools that can improve call quality, organization, and accessibility.

Enhanced calling features:

- **Call waiting**: Accept second calls without ending the first
- **Conference calling**: Merge multiple calls into group conversations
- **Call forwarding**: Redirect calls to another number when unavailable
- **Voicemail transcription**: Read voicemail messages as text

Setting up visual voicemail:

1. Open Phone app
2. Tap three dots menu > Settings
3. Select "Voicemail"

4. Follow carrier-specific setup instructions
5. Enable transcription if available

Speed dial simplifies calling your most important contacts:

Creating speed dial shortcuts:

1. Open Phone app
2. Tap "Keypad" tab
3. Tap three dots menu > "Speed dial numbers"
4. Assign numbers 2-9 to important contacts
5. Hold the assigned number to call directly

The Messages app handles both SMS text messages and RCS (Rich Communication Services) messages, which offer enhanced features when both parties have compatible phones.

RCS message features:

- Read receipts showing when messages are seen
- Typing indicators showing when someone is responding
- High-quality photo and video sharing
- Group messaging with better organization

Message organization tools:

1. Pin important conversations to the top
2. Archive old conversations to reduce clutter
3. Create conversation categories (Personal, Work, etc.)
4. Use search to find specific messages quickly

Voice message recording:

1. Open a conversation in Messages
2. Hold down the microphone icon
3. Speak your message clearly
4. Release to send automatically

NFC and Samsung Pay: Real-World Usage Scenarios

Near Field Communication (NFC) enables your phone to interact with compatible devices and payment terminals through simple tapping motions. Samsung Pay leverages this technology for secure, convenient transactions.

Enabling NFC:

1. Go to Settings > Connections
2. Toggle "NFC and contactless payments" on
3. Ensure "Samsung Pay" is set as default payment app

Setting up Samsung Pay:

1. Open Samsung Pay app (or download from Galaxy Store)
2. Sign in with Samsung account
3. Add your fingerprint for security
4. Create a 4-digit PIN as backup
5. Add credit/debit cards using camera or manual entry

Adding cards to Samsung Pay:

1. Open Samsung Pay
2. Tap "Add card"
3. Choose "Credit/Debit card"
4. Use camera to scan card or enter details manually
5. Verify through your bank's authentication process

Making payments with Samsung Pay:

1. Wake your phone screen
2. Swipe up from bottom edge or open Samsung Pay
3. Select desired card
4. Authenticate with fingerprint or PIN
5. Hold phone back against payment terminal
6. Wait for confirmation vibration and sound

Real-world payment scenarios:

- **Grocery stores**: Works at most major chains (Walmart, Target, Kroger)
- **Gas stations**: Tap at pump terminals for quick payment
- **Restaurants**: Many now accept contactless payment at table
- **Public transportation**: Some cities accept phone payments for buses/trains
- **Coffee shops**: Skip lines with mobile payment at Starbucks, etc.

NFC beyond payments:

- Share Wi-Fi passwords by tapping phones together
- Transfer photos between compatible devices
- Connect to Bluetooth speakers that support NFC pairing
- Access information from NFC tags in public places

Hotspot and Tethering: Making Your Phone a Router

Your Galaxy A16 5G can share its cellular internet connection with other devices, effectively becoming a portable Wi-Fi router. This feature proves invaluable when traveling or during home internet outages.

Setting up Mobile Hotspot:

1. Go to Settings > Connections > Mobile Hotspot and Tethering
2. Tap "Mobile Hotspot"
3. Toggle the feature on
4. Note the network name and password displayed
5. Customize settings if desired

Connecting devices to your hotspot:

1. On the device needing internet, open Wi-Fi settings
2. Look for your phone's hotspot name in available networks
3. Enter the password shown on your phone

4. Connect and verify internet access

Hotspot customization options:

- **Network name**: Change from default to something recognizable
- **Password**: Create memorable but secure password (minimum 8 characters)
- **Security type**: Keep as WPA3 for best protection
- **Band**: Use 2.4GHz for better range, 5GHz for faster speeds

Data usage management: Your cellular plan's data limits apply to hotspot usage. Monitor consumption to avoid overage charges:

1. Check data usage: Settings > Connections > Data usage
2. Set usage alerts: Tap "Billing cycle and data warning"
3. Enable data limit notifications
4. Consider unlimited plans if using hotspot frequently

Practical hotspot scenarios:

- **Travel**: Provide internet for tablets, laptops during trips
- **Home backup**: Maintain connectivity during broadband outages
- **Family sharing**: Give grandchildren internet access during visits
- **Work situations**: Support remote work when primary internet fails

Battery and performance considerations:

- Hotspot usage drains battery quickly - keep charger handy
- Connection speed depends on cellular signal strength
- Limit connected devices to 3-4 for best performance
- Turn off hotspot when not needed to preserve battery

Emergency Features That Could Save Your Life

The Galaxy A16 5G includes several emergency features designed to help in crisis situations, from medical emergencies to natural disasters. Understanding and configuring these features beforehand ensures they're available when needed most.

Emergency SOS activation:

1. Press Side button rapidly 5 times
2. Phone automatically calls emergency services
3. Sends location information to emergency contacts
4. Continues sharing location for specified duration

Setting up Emergency SOS:

1. Go to Settings > Safety and emergency > Emergency SOS
2. Enable "Call emergency services"
3. Add emergency contacts (minimum 2 recommended)
4. Choose whether to send photos/audio with emergency alerts

5. Practice the activation method with 911 dispatcher awareness

Emergency contacts configuration:

1. Go to Settings > Safety and emergency > Emergency contacts
2. Tap "Add contact"
3. Select from your contacts list
4. Choose relationship type
5. Verify phone numbers are current

Medical information setup: This information becomes accessible from the lock screen during emergencies:

1. Go to Settings > Safety and emergency > Medical info
2. Add critical information:
    - Blood type
    - Allergies
    - Current medications
    - Medical conditions
    - Emergency contact information

Location sharing during emergencies:

1. Enable "Enhanced 911" in Safety settings
2. Allow location access for emergency services
3. Set duration for automatic location sharing (1-24 hours)
4. Test with trusted contacts using "Share location" feature

Wireless Emergency Alerts: Your phone receives government emergency broadcasts automatically:

- **Presidential alerts**: Cannot be disabled, highest priority
- **Imminent threats**: Severe weather, terrorist attacks
- **AMBER alerts**: Child abduction notifications
- **Public safety messages**: Local emergency information

Customizing emergency alerts:

1. Go to Settings > Safety and emergency > Wireless emergency alerts
2. Choose which alert types to receive
3. Enable "Alert reminder" for repeated notifications
4. Set vibration and sound preferences

Emergency flashlight access:

- Double-press Side button when customized for flashlight
- Swipe down from top of screen, tap flashlight icon
- Say "Hey Google, turn on flashlight" for voice activation

Offline emergency preparedness:

- Download offline maps of your area before emergencies
- Save important phone numbers in contacts, not just favorites
- Keep phone charged above 50% when severe weather is forecast
- Know how to enable "Emergency mode" to extend battery life drastically

These emergency features work best when family members also understand them. Share this information with adult children or caregivers who might need to assist you during a crisis.

CHAPTER 6: APPS, PERFORMANCE, AND STORAGE MANAGEMENT

Managing your Galaxy A16 5G effectively means understanding which apps deserve space on your device and which ones simply create clutter. Samsung pre-installs dozens of apps, many of which you'll never use but that continue consuming storage space and system resources in the background. The difference between a phone that feels snappy and responsive versus one that seems sluggish often comes down to thoughtful app management and storage optimization.

Performance and storage issues typically develop gradually over months of use, making them easy to ignore until they become genuinely frustrating. This chapter provides practical strategies for maintaining your phone's performance from day one, preventing problems rather than fixing them after they occur. You'll learn to distinguish between essential apps and digital bloatware, implement storage strategies that actually work long-term, and configure settings that maximize both performance and battery life.

Pre-installed Apps: Keep, Disable, or Uninstall Guide

Samsung installs numerous apps on your A16 5G, creating immediate decisions about what to keep, disable, or remove entirely. Understanding the purpose and value of each category helps streamline your device.

Essential apps to keep:

- **Phone**: Core calling functionality
- **Messages**: Text messaging
- **Camera**: Photo and video capture
- **Gallery**: Photo management and editing
- **Settings**: System configuration
- **Contacts**: Address book management
- **Samsung Internet**: Web browsing (often better than Chrome on Samsung devices)
- **Samsung Notes**: Note-taking with stylus support

Samsung apps worth evaluating:

- **Samsung Health**: Comprehensive fitness tracking, useful if you want health monitoring
- **Samsung Pay**: Contactless payments, convenient once set up
- **Galaxy Store**: Samsung-specific apps and themes
- **Samsung Calendar**: Integrates well with Samsung ecosystem
- **My Files**: File management with good organization tools

Apps you can safely disable:

- **Facebook** (if pre-installed): Heavy resource usage, available from Play Store if needed
- **Microsoft Office apps**: Unless you specifically use them
- **Samsung TV Plus**: Streaming service you may not need
- **Galaxy Wearable**: Only needed if you own Samsung smartwatch
- **Samsung Kids**: Parental controls app for child users

Step-by-step app removal process:

1. Go to Settings > Apps
2. Find the app you want to remove
3. Tap the app name
4. Choose from available options:
   - **Uninstall**: Completely removes app (best option)
   - **Disable**: Hides app and stops it running
   - **Force stop**: Temporarily stops app until next restart

Google apps assessment:

- **Gmail**: Keep if you use Gmail email
- **Google Maps**: Excellent navigation, worth keeping
- **YouTube**: Popular video platform
- **Chrome**: Alternative browser to Samsung Internet
- **Google Photos**: Cloud photo backup (competes with Samsung Cloud)
- **Google Pay**: Alternative to Samsung Pay
- **Google Drive**: Cloud storage service

Carrier-installed apps: Your cellular carrier may install additional apps that are often unnecessary:

- Carrier-specific navigation apps (when Google Maps works better)
- Streaming services you don't subscribe to
- Carrier payment apps (when Samsung Pay or Google Pay work better)
- Insurance or protection apps you didn't request

Performance Optimization for Smooth Daily Use

Maintaining smooth performance requires regular attention to several key areas that affect how quickly your phone responds to commands and switches between apps.

Device Care optimization:

1. Go to Settings > Device care
2. Tap "Optimize now" for automatic cleanup
3. Review suggested optimizations
4. Enable "Auto optimization" for weekly maintenance

Memory management: Your A16 5G includes 4GB or 6GB of RAM depending on model. Efficient memory usage keeps apps running smoothly:

Manual memory cleanup:

1. Recent apps button (or swipe up and hold)
2. Tap "Close all" to clear unnecessary background apps
3. Keep frequently used apps running for faster access

Background app limits:

1. Settings > Device care > Battery > Background usage limits
2. Enable "Put unused apps to sleep"
3. Add rarely used apps to "Deep sleeping apps" list
4. Allow important apps to run unrestricted

Animation and visual effects: Reducing animations makes the interface feel more responsive:

1. Settings > Accessibility > Visibility enhancements
2. Enable "Remove animations"
3. Alternative: Settings > Developer options > Animation scale (set to 0.5x)

Storage impact on performance: Keep at least 10-15% of storage free for optimal performance:

- **Below 85% full**: Normal performance
- **85-95% full**: Noticeable slowdowns
- **Above 95% full**: Significant performance issues

Network optimization:

1. Settings > Connections > Wi-Fi > Advanced
2. Enable "Switch to mobile data" for seamless transitions
3. Turn off "Wi-Fi scanning" if experiencing connectivity issues

Regular maintenance schedule:

- **Daily**: Close unused apps before bed
- **Weekly**: Run Device care optimization
- **Monthly**: Clear cache for heavy-use apps
- **Quarterly**: Review and remove unused apps

Storage Management Strategies That Actually Work

The Galaxy A16 5G comes with either 128GB or 256GB of internal storage, which sounds like plenty until you start accumulating photos, videos, and app data over time.

Storage breakdown understanding:

1. Settings > Device care > Storage
2. Review categories showing space usage:
    - **Apps**: Installed applications and their data
    - **Images**: Photos and screenshots
    - **Videos**: Recorded and downloaded videos
    - **Audio**: Music, ringtones, voice recordings
    - **Documents**: PDFs, text files, downloads

Photo and video management: Photos typically consume the most storage space over time:

Cloud backup strategy:

1. Enable Samsung Cloud or Google Photos backup
2. Settings > Accounts and backup > Samsung Cloud
3. Turn on "Gallery" sync
4. Choose "Optimize storage" to keep smaller local copies

Local photo cleanup:

1. Gallery app > Menu > Recycle bin
2. Empty recycle bin monthly
3. Delete duplicate photos using Gallery's built-in detection
4. Remove blurry or unwanted photos immediately after taking them

App data management: Apps accumulate cache and data over time:

Cache clearing process:

1. Settings > Apps
2. Select app with high storage usage
3. Tap "Storage"
4. Choose "Clear cache" (safe) or "Clear data" (removes app settings)

Large app identification:

1. Settings > Device care > Storage
2. Tap "Apps"
3. Sort by size to find storage-heavy apps
4. Consider alternatives or removal for unused large apps

Downloads folder cleanup:

1. My Files app > Internal storage > Download
2. Delete old PDF files, images, documents
3. Move important files to organized folders
4. Empty Downloads folder monthly

microSD card utilization: If your model supports microSD cards:

1. Purchase high-speed card (Class 10 or better)
2. Settings > Device care > Storage
3. Transfer photos and videos to SD card
4. Set camera to save directly to SD card

Battery Life: Real-World Tips for All-Day Usage

The A16 5G's 5000mAh battery provides excellent longevity, but several factors affect how long it lasts between charges.

Battery usage analysis:

1. Settings > Device care > Battery

2. Review "Battery usage" to identify power-hungry apps
3. Check "Screen on time" for realistic usage metrics

Power saving modes: Regular power saving:

- Reduces CPU performance slightly
- Limits background app activity
- Extends battery life by 10-20%

Maximum power saving:

- Switches to basic interface
- Limits app selection severely
- Can extend battery life for hours when critical

Activation steps:

1. Settings > Device care > Battery
2. Select desired power saving mode
3. Customize restrictions if needed

Display optimization for battery:

- **Brightness**: Use adaptive brightness or manual setting around 40-60%
- **Screen timeout**: Set to 1-2 minutes maximum
- **Dark mode**: Saves battery on AMOLED displays
- **Refresh rate**: Use 60Hz instead of 90Hz for longer battery life

Location services management:

1. Settings > Location
2. Turn off for apps that don't need location
3. Set precision to "Improve accuracy" only when needed
4. Disable "Wi-Fi and Bluetooth scanning"

Background app restrictions: Automatic restrictions:

1. Settings > Device care > Battery > Background usage limits
2. Enable "Put unused apps to sleep"
3. Add social media apps to "Deep sleeping apps"

Manual app optimization:

1. Settings > Apps
2. Select battery-heavy app
3. Tap "Battery"
4. Choose "Optimize battery usage"

Charging best practices:

- **Avoid 0-100% cycles**: Charge between 20-80% when possible
- **Overnight charging**: Modern phones stop charging at 100%, so it's safe
- **Heat management**: Avoid charging in hot environments
- **Cable quality**: Use original or certified USB-C cables

Real-world battery expectations:

- **Light usage**: 2+ days (calls, texts, minimal apps)
- **Moderate usage**: 1.5 days (social media, photos, navigation)
- **Heavy usage**: Full day (gaming, video streaming, GPS)

Security and Privacy Settings You Can't Ignore

Protecting your personal information requires configuring several security layers that work together to prevent unauthorized access and data theft.

Lock screen security:

1. Settings > Lock screen > Screen lock type
2. Choose PIN, password, or biometric options
3. Enable "Lock automatically" after 5 seconds
4. Turn on "Lock network and security"

Biometric security setup: Fingerprint configuration:

1. Settings > Biometrics and security > Fingerprints
2. Add multiple fingerprints (thumb and index finger)
3. Enable "Fingerprint unlock"
4. Test recognition reliability

Face recognition setup:

1. Settings > Biometrics and security > Face recognition
2. Register in good lighting conditions
3. Add alternative appearance if you wear glasses

4. Understand limitations (less secure than fingerprint)

App permissions management: Permission review process:

1. Settings > Apps > Permission manager
2. Review each permission category:
   - **Camera**: Only photography and video call apps
   - **Microphone**: Voice assistants, calling apps
   - **Location**: Maps, weather, delivery apps
   - **Contacts**: Communication and social apps
   - **Storage**: File managers, photo editors

Privacy settings configuration:

1. Settings > Privacy
2. Turn off "Ads personalization"
3. Limit "Usage and diagnostics" data sharing
4. Review "Permission manager" for overprivileged apps

Samsung account security:

1. Two-factor authentication setup
2. Regular password updates
3. Review connected devices periodically
4. Monitor account activity for suspicious access

Network security: Wi-Fi protection:

- Avoid public Wi-Fi for sensitive activities
- Use "Private DNS" in network settings
- Enable "Randomize MAC address" for privacy

App installation security:

1. Settings > Apps > Special access > Install unknown apps
2. Disable for all apps except trusted sources
3. Keep "Play Protect" enabled in Google Play Store
4. Review app permissions before installation

Data backup and recovery:

1. Settings > Accounts and backup > Samsung Cloud
2. Enable automatic backup for important data
3. Create local backups before major updates
4. Test restore process to verify backup integrity

Security monitoring:

1. Settings > Device care > Security
2. Run weekly malware scans
3. Keep software updated automatically
4. Monitor unusual battery drain or performance issues

CHAPTER 7: SAMSUNG ECOSYSTEM INTEGRATION

Samsung has built an interconnected ecosystem of services designed to work seamlessly across their devices, from smartphones to tablets to smartwatches. For seniors, this ecosystem can either simplify your digital life by keeping everything synchronized and accessible, or create confusion with overlapping services that duplicate what Google already provides. The key is understanding which Samsung services genuinely add value versus those that simply create another account to manage.

The Galaxy A16 5G serves as your gateway into Samsung's ecosystem, but you're not required to use every service they offer. This chapter helps you make informed decisions about which Samsung services align with your actual needs and usage patterns, rather than simply accepting everything because it's pre-installed.

Samsung Account: Worth It or Marketing Hype?

A Samsung account provides genuine benefits that extend beyond marketing convenience, particularly for device backup, app purchases, and cross-device synchronization.

Essential Samsung account benefits:

- Automatic backup of device settings, contacts, and app data
- Find My Mobile service for locating lost devices
- Samsung Pay setup and transaction history
- Galaxy Store app purchases and updates
- Samsung Cloud storage (15GB free)
- Device warranty and support tracking

Account setup process:

1. Settings > Accounts and backup > Add account > Samsung account
2. Choose "Create account" or sign in with existing credentials
3. Verify email address through confirmation link
4. Set up two-factor authentication for security
5. Choose data sync preferences

Data syncing configuration:

1. Settings > Accounts and backup > Samsung account
2. Select "Sync account"
3. Enable syncing for desired categories:
   - **Contacts**: Essential for backup
   - **Calendar**: Keeps appointments synchronized
   - **Samsung Notes**: Syncs across devices
   - **Internet**: Bookmarks and passwords
   - **Gallery**: Photo backup to Samsung Cloud

Privacy and data sharing controls:

1. Samsung account settings > Privacy
2. Disable "Customization Service" if you prefer less targeted content
3. Turn off "Analytics" unless you want to help improve Samsung services
4. Review "Marketing" preferences and disable unwanted communications

When Samsung account isn't necessary:

- If you primarily use Google services (Gmail, Google Photos, Google Drive)
- When you only plan to use your phone for basic functions
- If managing multiple accounts feels overwhelming
- When you prefer Apple or Microsoft ecosystems

Galaxy Store vs Google Play: Which Apps to Get Where

Both app stores serve the A16 5G, but they excel in different areas and offer distinct advantages depending on your needs.

Galaxy Store advantages:

- Samsung-optimized apps designed specifically for Galaxy devices
- Good Lock customization tools and plugins
- Samsung themes and wallpapers

- Apps that integrate deeply with Samsung hardware features
- Sometimes offers free premium apps as promotions

Google Play Store advantages:

- Larger app selection with virtually every popular app
- More frequent app updates from developers
- Better app discovery and recommendation system
- Familiar interface if you've used Android before
- More comprehensive user reviews and ratings

Apps to get from Galaxy Store:

- **Samsung Internet**: Browser optimized for Samsung devices
- **Samsung Notes**: Enhanced with S Pen features on compatible devices
- **Samsung Health**: Integrates with Samsung wearables
- **Good Lock**: Advanced customization options
- **Samsung Themes**: Visual customization for your device
- **Samsung calculator**: Designed to match Samsung interface

Apps to get from Google Play:

- **Social media apps**: Facebook, Instagram, Twitter, TikTok
- **Streaming services**: Netflix, YouTube, Spotify, Pandora
- **Communication**: WhatsApp, Telegram, Skype
- **Banking and finance**: Your bank's official app, PayPal, Venmo

- **Productivity**: Microsoft Office, Adobe apps, Dropbox
- **Games**: Most mobile games are available here first

Managing updates from both stores:

1. Galaxy Store: Menu > Settings > Auto update apps
2. Google Play: Profile > Settings > Network preferences > Auto-update apps
3. Choose "Over Wi-Fi only" to avoid cellular data charges

Samsung Health, Notes, and Productivity Apps Deep Dive

Samsung's productivity apps offer features specifically designed for their hardware, though they compete directly with Google's alternatives.

Samsung Health comprehensive setup:

1. Open Samsung Health app
2. Complete initial profile setup with accurate personal information
3. Connect compatible devices (smartwatch, fitness tracker)
4. Set realistic daily goals for steps, activity, sleep

Key Samsung Health features:

- **Step tracking**: Uses phone's built-in sensors automatically
- **Heart rate monitoring**: Camera-based measurement

- **Sleep tracking**: When phone is placed on nightstand
- **Food logging**: Calorie and nutrition tracking
- **Exercise tracking**: Manual or automatic workout detection

Samsung Notes advantages over Google Keep:

- Better organization with folders and categories
- Handwriting recognition and conversion to text
- Audio recording synchronized with written notes
- PDF annotation capabilities
- More formatting options for text notes

Samsung Notes organization strategy:

1. Create folders for different note categories (Medical, Shopping, Ideas)
2. Use tags for easy searching across folders
3. Pin important notes to top of lists
4. Enable sync with Samsung Cloud for backup

Samsung Calendar vs Google Calendar: Samsung Calendar benefits:

- Integrates with Samsung Health for fitness goals
- Weather information in daily view
- More customizable widget options
- Works offline with local storage

Google Calendar benefits:

- Better integration with Gmail and other Google services
- More robust sharing capabilities
- Superior web interface for computer access
- Better cross-platform compatibility

Smart Switch and Data Migration Done Right

Smart Switch simplifies transferring data from your old phone to the Galaxy A16 5G, supporting both Android and iPhone migrations.

Pre-migration preparation:

1. Ensure old phone has at least 50% battery charge
2. Connect both devices to Wi-Fi for faster transfer
3. Update Smart Switch app on both devices if Android-to-Android
4. Back up old phone to cloud services as additional safeguard

Android to Samsung transfer:

1. Open Smart Switch on both devices
2. Select transfer method:
    - **Wireless**: Slower but more convenient
    - **Cable**: Faster, requires USB-C to USB adapter
3. Choose "Send data" on old phone, "Receive data" on A16 5G
4. Select data categories to transfer
5. Begin transfer and wait for completion

iPhone to Samsung transfer:

1. Download Smart Switch on A16 5G
2. Use Lightning to USB-C adapter for cable connection
3. Trust the connection on iPhone when prompted
4. Select data types available for transfer:
   - **Contacts**: Transfers completely
   - **Photos**: Transfers but may need organization
   - **Calendar**: Syncs with Samsung Calendar
   - **Messages**: Limited transfer capability

What transfers successfully:

- Contacts with phone numbers and email addresses
- Photos and videos (may take several hours for large collections)
- Calendar appointments and events
- Some app data (varies by app)
- Music files stored locally on device

What doesn't transfer well:

- App login credentials (you'll need to sign in again)
- iOS-specific app data to Android alternatives
- FaceTime history or iMessage conversations
- Apple-specific settings and preferences
- Some photo metadata and organization

Post-transfer cleanup:

1. Verify contacts transferred correctly
2. Check photo organization and create albums as needed
3. Re-download apps from appropriate app stores
4. Sign into accounts for email, social media, banking
5. Reconfigure notification preferences

Samsung Cloud vs Google Drive: Storage Strategy

Both services offer cloud storage, but they serve different purposes and work better for different types of content.

Samsung Cloud strengths:

- Seamless device backup and restoration
- Automatic sync of Samsung app data
- Gallery sync with intelligent organization
- Settings backup for easy device replacement
- Better integration with Samsung apps

Google Drive strengths:

- Larger free storage (15GB vs Samsung's 15GB)
- Better cross-platform compatibility
- Superior document collaboration features
- Integration with Google Workspace
- More third-party app compatibility

Optimal storage strategy: Use Samsung Cloud for:

- Device settings and configuration backup
- Samsung app data (Health, Notes, Calendar)
- Photo backup as primary or secondary option
- Contact synchronization across Samsung devices

Use Google Drive for:

- Document storage and sharing
- Cross-platform file access
- Collaboration on spreadsheets and documents
- Backup for non-Samsung apps
- Large file storage and sharing

Samsung Cloud setup:

1. Settings > Accounts and backup > Samsung Cloud
2. Sign in with Samsung account
3. Configure backup settings:
   - **Apps**: Select which app data to backup
   - **Settings**: System preferences and configurations
   - **Gallery**: Photo and video backup options
4. Enable "Auto backup" for hands-off operation

Storage space management:

1. Monitor usage in Samsung Cloud settings
2. Delete old device backups periodically
3. Use "Optimize storage" for photos to save space
4. Consider upgrading storage if you exceed free tier

Backup verification:

1. Periodically check that backups are completing successfully
2. Test restore process on less critical data
3. Maintain local backups of irreplaceable photos/videos
4. Use both services for redundancy on important data

Cost comparison for additional storage:

- **Samsung Cloud**: $0.99/month for 50GB, $2.99/month for 200GB
- **Google Drive**: $1.99/month for 100GB, $2.99/month for 200GB

Choose based on which ecosystem you use more frequently and which offers better value for your specific storage needs.

CHAPTER 8: ADVANCED FEATURES AND HIDDEN GEMS

Your Galaxy A16 5G contains powerful features that remain hidden beneath the surface of everyday use. While Samsung designed the phone to work excellently with default settings, understanding these advanced capabilities can transform your device from a simple communication tool into a sophisticated personal assistant. These features aren't just for technology enthusiasts – many solve practical problems that seniors face daily, from vision challenges to repetitive tasks.

This chapter reveals genuinely useful advanced features while avoiding overly technical modifications that could cause problems. You'll discover automation tools that can simplify your daily routine, accessibility features that improve usability regardless of physical limitations, and productivity enhancements that make your phone work smarter, not harder.

Developer Options and Power User Tweaks

Developer options unlock advanced settings normally hidden from regular users. While intimidating in name, several options provide practical benefits.

Enabling Developer Options:

1. Settings > About phone > Software information
2. Tap "Build number" seven times rapidly
3. Enter your lock screen PIN/password when prompted
4. Return to main Settings menu
5. Find "Developer options" near bottom of list

Useful Developer Options for seniors:

Animation speed adjustment:

- Window animation scale: Set to 0.5x for snappier interface
- Transition animation scale: Set to 0.5x for faster app switching
- Animator duration scale: Set to 0.5x for quicker responses

Display improvements:

- Force 90Hz refresh rate: Smoother scrolling (impacts battery)
- Smallest width: Increase to 480dp for more content on screen

- Secondary display cutout: Hide camera notch if it bothers you

Performance tweaks:

- Background process limit: Set to "At most 3 processes" for better performance
- Don't keep activities: Forces apps to fully reload (use only if experiencing issues)

Caution areas to avoid:

- USB debugging settings
- Mock location apps
- Hardware acceleration options
- System UI tuner modifications

Accessibility Features That Benefit Everyone

Samsung's accessibility features help users with various challenges but often improve the experience for all users.

Vision enhancements: High contrast and visibility:

1. Settings > Accessibility > Visibility enhancements
2. Enable "High contrast text" for better readability
3. Turn on "Remove animations" for clearer interface transitions
4. Use "Color adjustment" if you have difficulty distinguishing colors

Magnification tools:

- **Magnification shortcut**: Triple-tap screen to zoom
- **Magnifier**: Use camera as magnifying glass for small text
- **Large mouse/trackpad pointer**: Easier to see cursor

Hearing enhancements: Sound and vibration improvements:

1. Settings > Accessibility > Hearing enhancements
2. Enable "Sound amplifier" for clearer audio through headphones
3. Turn on "Live Caption" for automatic subtitle generation
4. Use "Sound detectors" for doorbell/baby crying alerts

Interaction improvements: Touch and motor assistance:

- **Touch and hold delay**: Extend time needed for long presses
- **Tap duration**: Adjust how long taps must be held
- **Ignore repeated touches**: Prevent accidental double-taps
- **Sticky keys**: Use modifier keys without holding them

Voice Access setup:

1. Download Voice Access from Google Play
2. Settings > Accessibility > Voice Access
3. Follow tutorial for voice commands
4. Use for hands-free phone operation

Universal benefits of accessibility features:

- Larger text helps in bright sunlight or when tired
- High contrast reduces eye strain during extended use
- Voice commands useful when hands are occupied
- Magnification helpful for reading fine print anywhere

Automation with Modes and Routines

Modes and Routines automate repetitive tasks and adjust settings based on time, location, or activities.

Understanding Modes vs Routines:

- **Modes**: Preset collections of settings for specific situations
- **Routines**: Custom automated actions triggered by conditions

Setting up useful Modes:

1. Settings > Modes and Routines > Modes
2. Available preset modes:
    - **Sleep**: Enables Do Not Disturb, reduces brightness
    - **Work**: Silences personal notifications, enables work apps
    - **Exercise**: Activates Samsung Health, disables non-essential notifications
    - **Driving**: Enables hands-free features, reads messages aloud

Creating custom Routines: Morning routine example:

1. Settings > Modes and Routines > Routines
2. Tap "+" to create new routine
3. Set trigger: Time (7:00 AM weekdays)
4. Add actions:
   - Turn off Do Not Disturb
   - Set volume to 70%
   - Open weather app
   - Read calendar appointments aloud

Bedtime routine:

- Trigger: Time (9:00 PM)
- Actions: Enable Do Not Disturb, dim screen, turn on blue light filter

Location-based routines:

- **Home arrival**: Connect to Wi-Fi, disable mobile data, turn on smart lights
- **Doctor's office**: Silence phone, open insurance app, set 1-hour Do Not Disturb

Practical routine ideas:

- **Medication reminder**: Daily alert with pill tracker app
- **Exercise time**: Open fitness app, connect Bluetooth headphones
- **Grocery shopping**: Open shopping list, enable location services
- **Church/theater**: Complete silence mode with vibration

Screen Recording, Screenshots, and Sharing Mastery

Capturing and sharing screen content helps communicate with family, save important information, and create helpful references.

Screenshot methods: Button combination:

1. Press Side button + Volume Down simultaneously
2. Hold briefly until capture sound/animation
3. Screenshot saves to Gallery automatically

Palm swipe capture:

1. Settings > Advanced features > Motions and gestures
2. Enable "Palm swipe to capture"
3. Swipe hand edge across screen left to right

Screenshot editing tools: After taking screenshot, toolbar appears with options:

- **Scroll capture**: Capture long web pages or conversations
- **Draw**: Add arrows, text, highlights to image
- **Crop**: Remove unwanted portions
- **Share**: Send immediately via text, email, or social media

Screen recording setup:

1. Swipe down from top of screen twice
2. Look for "Screen recorder" in quick settings

3. If not visible: Settings > Advanced features > Screenshots and screen recorder
4. Enable "Show Screen recorder"

Screen recording process:

1. Tap Screen recorder icon in quick settings
2. Choose audio source:
    - **No sound**: Silent recording
    - **Media sounds**: Capture app audio
    - **Media and microphone**: Include your voice
3. Tap "Start recording"
4. Navigate to content you want to record
5. Tap red recording icon to stop

Practical recording uses:

- Demonstrate app problems to tech support
- Save video instructions for later reference
- Record video calls with grandchildren
- Capture social media content before it disappears

Sharing options mastery: Quick Share (Samsung devices):

1. Select content to share
2. Tap Share button
3. Choose "Quick Share" at top of list
4. Select nearby Samsung device

Link sharing for large files:

1. Select photos/videos to share
2. Tap Share > Create link
3. Set expiration time and access permissions
4. Share generated link via text or email

Gaming Performance and Game Booster Reality

Game Booster optimizes performance for mobile gaming, though benefits vary by game type and device usage.

Game Booster activation:

1. Settings > Advanced features > Game Booster
2. Enable "Game Booster"
3. Choose performance level:
    - **Focus on performance**: Maximum speed, higher battery drain
    - **Balanced**: Moderate performance improvement
    - **Focus on battery**: Extended gaming time, reduced performance

Realistic Game Booster benefits: Noticeable improvements:

- Reduced notification interruptions during gaming
- Priority CPU allocation for smoother gameplay
- Background app suspension saves battery
- Gaming toolbar for screenshots and recording

Limited improvements:

- Graphics quality (hardware dependent)
- Loading times (storage speed dependent)
- Network lag (internet connection dependent)

Game Booster panel features: During gaming, swipe from screen edge to access:

- **Lock navigation buttons**: Prevent accidental exits
- **Block notifications**: Temporary Do Not Disturb
- **Monitor performance**: Check temperature and memory usage
- **Screenshot/record**: Capture gaming moments

Gaming optimization tips: Performance improvements:

- Close background apps before gaming
- Enable airplane mode for offline games to save battery
- Use wired headphones to reduce Bluetooth audio lag
- Charge device while gaming for consistent performance

Battery conservation:

- Lower screen brightness for longer gaming sessions
- Disable mobile data if using Wi-Fi
- Close social media apps running in background
- Use balanced Game Booster mode instead of performance mode

Popular senior-friendly games that benefit:

- **Solitaire/card games**: Smooth animation improvements
- **Puzzle games**: Better touch responsiveness
- **Word games**: Reduced lag during letter selection
- **Casual strategy games**: Improved menu navigation

When Game Booster isn't helpful:

- Simple apps like calculator or notes
- Video streaming (Netflix, YouTube)
- Basic photography apps
- Calling and messaging

Game Booster works best with resource-intensive games. For light gaming or basic apps, the performance impact is minimal, and you might prefer leaving it disabled to conserve battery life.

CHAPTER 9: TROUBLESHOOTING AND MAINTENANCE

Even the most reliable smartphones encounter occasional issues, and the Galaxy A16 5G is no exception. The difference between a minor inconvenience and major frustration often lies in knowing how to diagnose problems correctly and apply appropriate solutions. Most smartphone issues stem from software conflicts, storage problems, or simple configuration errors rather than hardware failures, meaning you can resolve many problems yourself without expensive repair visits.

Preventive maintenance significantly extends your phone's lifespan and performance. This chapter provides practical troubleshooting steps arranged from simplest to most comprehensive, helping you determine when a quick fix will suffice versus when professional assistance becomes necessary. You'll learn to distinguish between normal aging behaviors and genuine problems requiring intervention.

Common Problems and Realistic Solutions

Phone feels slow or unresponsive:

Immediate solutions:

1. Close all recent apps: Recent apps button → "Close all"
2. Restart the device: Hold Side button → "Restart"
3. Clear storage space if below 15% available

If problem persists:

1. Settings → Device care → "Optimize now"
2. Check for misbehaving apps: Settings → Device care → Battery → Battery usage
3. Disable unused apps: Settings → Apps → Select app → "Disable"

Apps crashing or not opening:

Single app problems:

1. Settings → Apps → Select problematic app
2. Tap "Force stop" → "Clear cache"
3. If still problematic: "Clear data" (removes app settings)
4. Last resort: Uninstall and reinstall from app store

Multiple app crashes:

- Usually indicates system-level issue requiring restart or software update

Wi-Fi connection problems:

Basic troubleshooting:

1. Toggle Wi-Fi off and on: Settings → Connections → Wi-Fi
2. "Forget" and reconnect to network
3. Restart router by unplugging 30 seconds
4. Check if other devices connect successfully to same network

Advanced solutions:

1. Settings → General management → Reset → "Reset network settings"
2. Change DNS settings: Wi-Fi → Advanced → IP settings → Static
3. Use Google DNS: 8.8.8.8 and 8.8.4.4

Battery draining too quickly:

Diagnostic steps:

1. Settings → Device care → Battery → "Battery usage"
2. Identify apps consuming excessive power
3. Check screen-on time (normal: 4-8 hours depending on usage)

Solutions by cause:

- **High screen usage**: Reduce brightness, shorter timeout
- **Background apps**: Enable power saving mode, restrict background activity
- **Poor signal**: Use airplane mode in dead zones, enable Wi-Fi calling
- **Old battery**: Consider professional battery replacement after 2+ years

Bluetooth connection issues:

Standard fixes:

1. Turn Bluetooth off/on in quick settings
2. "Forget" problematic device and re-pair
3. Clear Bluetooth cache: Settings → Apps → Bluetooth → Storage → "Clear cache"
4. Restart both devices

Overheating problems:

Immediate actions:

- Remove phone case temporarily
- Close resource-intensive apps
- Move to cooler environment
- Stop charging if device is hot

Prevention:

- Avoid direct sunlight during use
- Don't leave in hot cars
- Close games/video apps when not in use
- Use original charger only

Storage full warnings:

Quick cleanup:

1. Empty recycle bin: Gallery → Menu → Recycle bin → "Empty"
2. Clear Downloads folder: My Files → Downloads
3. Remove large apps: Settings → Apps → Sort by size

Thorough cleanup:

1. Settings → Device care → Storage → "Clean now"
2. Review and delete duplicate photos
3. Move photos/videos to cloud storage
4. Uninstall unused apps

When to Restart, Reset, or Seek Professional Help

Simple restart (try first):

- Apps running slowly
- Minor glitches or freezing

- After installing multiple apps
- Weekly maintenance

Forced restart: When phone becomes completely unresponsive:

1. Hold Side button + Volume Down for 10+ seconds
2. Release when Samsung logo appears
3. Wait for normal startup

When to consider factory reset:

- Multiple persistent problems after other solutions
- Phone significantly slower than when new
- Frequent app crashes across different apps
- Before selling or giving away device

Factory reset process:

1. Back up important data first
2. Settings → General management → Reset → "Factory data reset"
3. Read warnings carefully
4. Enter lock screen credentials
5. Confirm reset and wait for completion

Professional help indicators:

Hardware problems requiring repair:

- Cracked screen affecting touch sensitivity

- Camera producing consistently blurry images
- Charging port not working with multiple cables
- Phone randomly shutting off despite good battery
- Physical damage from drops or water
- Overheating even when idle

Software problems beyond DIY fixes:

- Boot loops (phone restarts continuously)
- Complete system crashes
- Factory reset doesn't resolve major issues
- Security concerns about malware

Battery Health and Charging Best Practices

Understanding battery degradation: Lithium batteries naturally lose capacity over time. Normal degradation:

- Year 1: 95-100% original capacity
- Year 2: 85-95% original capacity
- Year 3: 75-85% original capacity

Charging best practices:

Daily habits:

- Charge between 20-80% when convenient
- Avoid letting battery reach 0% regularly
- Overnight charging is safe (phone stops at 100%)
- Unplug when convenient, but don't stress about exact timing

Heat management:

- Don't charge in direct sunlight
- Remove thick cases during charging if phone gets warm
- Avoid wireless charging pads in hot cars
- Stop using phone if it becomes hot while charging

Battery protection settings:

1. Settings → Device care → Battery → "Battery protection"
2. Enable "Protect battery" to limit charge to 85%
3. Use during extended storage periods
4. Disable for daily use unless battery aging is concern

Charging equipment recommendations:

- Use original Samsung charger when available
- Certified USB-C cables (look for USB-IF logo)
- Avoid gas station or dollar store chargers
- Wireless chargers: Stick to reputable brands (Samsung, Anker, Belkin)

Signs of battery problems:

- Rapid drain (phone dies in few hours with minimal use)
- Won't charge past certain percentage
- Random shutoffs at 20%+ battery
- Extreme heat during charging
- Physical swelling (stop using immediately)

Software Updates: Timing and What to Expect

Update types:

Security updates (monthly):

- Small downloads (50-200MB)
- Install quickly (10-15 minutes)
- Safe to install immediately
- Fix security vulnerabilities

Feature updates (quarterly):

- Larger downloads (500MB-2GB)
- Longer installation (30-60 minutes)
- May change interface elements
- Consider waiting 1-2 weeks for bug reports

Major Android updates (yearly):

- Very large downloads (2-4GB)
- Significant installation time (1-2 hours)
- Major interface and feature changes
- Wait 2-4 weeks for stability confirmation

Update preparation:

1. Connect to Wi-Fi (avoid cellular data charges)
2. Charge battery above 50%
3. Back up important data

4. Close all apps before starting
5. Ensure 3+ GB free storage space

Manual update check:

1. Settings → Software update
2. Tap "Download and install"
3. Follow prompts if update available
4. Phone will restart multiple times during installation

Update timing strategy:

- Install security updates promptly
- Delay feature updates if phone working well
- Update before travel for latest features
- Avoid updates during busy periods (work deadlines, events)

Post-update issues: *Common temporary problems:*

- Slower performance first 24-48 hours (indexing)
- Increased battery drain initially
- Apps needing reconfiguration
- Interface changes requiring adjustment

When to worry:

- Persistent crashes after 1 week
- Major feature loss
- Significantly worse battery life after 1 month
- Apps completely stop working

Hardware Care and Longevity Tips

Screen protection:

- Tempered glass screen protectors ($10-20)
- Replace protectors when cracked
- Clean screen with microfiber cloth only
- Avoid alcohol-based cleaners

Physical handling:

- Use cases with raised edges around screen
- Two-handed operation when possible
- Avoid placing in back pockets
- Don't stack heavy items on top

Environmental protection: *Temperature management:*

- Avoid extended exposure below 32°F or above 95°F
- Don't leave in hot cars (interior temps reach 150°F+)
- Bring inside during extreme weather

Moisture protection:

- Wipe dry immediately after rain exposure
- Avoid steamy bathrooms during hot showers
- Don't charge if moisture in USB port
- Rice treatment myth: Use silica gel packets instead

Port and button maintenance:

- Clean USB-C port monthly with dry toothbrush
- Don't force cables into port
- Press buttons firmly but not aggressively
- Protect headphone jack with dust plugs if frequently used

Storage and transport:

- Dedicated phone pocket in purse/bag
- Avoid keys and coins in same pocket
- Use belt holsters for active work
- Consider neck straps for outdoor activities

Professional maintenance schedule:

- Annual checkup at carrier store or repair shop
- Battery replacement typically needed year 3-4
- Screen protector replacement as needed
- Case replacement when showing wear

Warning signs requiring immediate attention:

- Visible screen cracks
- Phone won't turn on
- Charging port damage
- Button stuck or unresponsive
- Any physical swelling or deformation

Long-term value preservation:

- Keep original box and accessories
- Maintain purchase receipts for warranty
- Document any repairs with receipts
- Regular cleaning maintains appearance
- Software updates extend useful life

CHAPTER 10: CUSTOMIZATION AND PERSONALIZATION

Making your Galaxy A16 5G feel uniquely yours goes beyond simply changing the wallpaper. Samsung provides extensive customization options that can improve both the aesthetic appeal and functional efficiency of your device. The key is understanding which modifications enhance your daily experience versus those that merely look different without adding practical value.

This chapter focuses on meaningful customization that solves real usability challenges while reflecting your personal preferences. From visual themes that reduce eye strain to sound profiles that ensure you never miss important calls, these modifications transform your phone from a generic device into a personalized tool that works exactly how you need it to.

Themes, Wallpapers, and Visual Customization

Accessing Samsung Themes:

1. Settings > Themes
2. Browse categories: Free, Premium, Recent
3. Preview themes before downloading
4. Apply instantly or schedule for later

Recommended theme categories for seniors:

- **High contrast themes**: Improve text readability
- **Large icon themes**: Easier targeting for touch
- **Simple themes**: Reduce visual clutter
- **Dark themes**: Reduce eye strain, save battery

Custom wallpaper setup:

1. Long-press home screen > Wallpapers and style
2. Choose source:
   - **Gallery**: Your personal photos
   - **Wallpaper services**: Samsung's collection
   - **Live wallpapers**: Animated backgrounds (drain battery)

Wallpaper best practices:

- Use high-contrast images for better icon visibility
- Avoid busy patterns that make text hard to read
- Consider different wallpapers for home and lock screens

- Test readability with white and dark text

Icon customization:

1. Settings > Themes > Icons
2. Options include:
    - **Rounded corners**: Softer appearance
    - **Sharp edges**: Traditional look
    - **Colorful**: Vibrant icon colors
    - **Monochrome**: Single color scheme

Always-On Display customization:

1. Settings > Lock screen > Always On Display
2. Choose clock styles, colors, and information displayed
3. Set schedule to save battery (example: 7 AM - 11 PM)
4. Add personal images or calendar information

Sound Profiles and Audio Enhancement

Creating custom sound profiles:

1. Settings > Modes and Routines > Modes
2. Create mode for different environments:
    - **Home**: Normal ringtone volume, notification sounds
    - **Sleep**: Calls only from contacts, no notifications
    - **Public**: Vibrate only, no sounds

Ringtone customization:

1. Settings > Sounds and vibration > Ringtone
2. Options:
    - **Samsung ringtones**: Pre-installed options
    - **My sounds**: Custom audio files
    - **Spotify**: Music streaming selections (requires premium)

Custom ringtone creation:

1. Choose audio file under 30 seconds
2. My Files > Internal storage > Ringtones folder
3. Copy desired audio file to this location
4. Select in ringtone settings

Audio enhancement settings:

1. Settings > Sounds and vibration > Sound quality and effects
2. Key features:
    - **Dolby Atmos**: Enhanced spatial audio
    - **Equalizer**: Adjust frequency responses
    - **Adapt sound**: Personalized audio profile
    - **UHQ upscaler**: Improve compressed audio quality

Notification sound strategy:

- **Calls**: Distinct, loud ringtone you'll recognize
- **Text messages**: Shorter, gentler tone
- **Email**: Subtle notification or silent
- **Apps**: Limit to essential apps only

Volume level optimization:

1. Settings > Sounds and vibration > Volume
2. Set different levels for:
   - **Media**: Music, videos, games
   - **Ringtone**: Incoming calls
   - **Notifications**: App alerts
   - **System**: Touch sounds, keyboard clicks

Keyboard Customization and Input Methods

Samsung Keyboard setup:

1. Settings > General management > Samsung Keyboard settings
2. Essential customizations:
   - **Languages and types**: Add needed languages
   - **Smart typing**: Predictive text, auto-correct
   - **Keyboard size and layout**: Adjust for comfort

Keyboard size adjustment:

1. Open keyboard in any text field
2. Tap gear icon > Size and transparency
3. Drag corners to resize
4. Test typing comfort with new size

One-handed keyboard mode:

1. Samsung Keyboard settings > Modes
2. Enable "One-handed operation"

3. Keyboard shrinks to left or right side
4. Useful for large hands or single-handed use

Alternative keyboard options:

- **Gboard** (Google): Excellent voice typing, extensive language support
- **SwiftKey** (Microsoft): Superior prediction, theme options
- **Voice typing**: Built-in speech-to-text for hands-free input

Voice typing optimization:

1. Keyboard > Microphone icon
2. Speak clearly at normal pace
3. Say punctuation: "period," "comma," "question mark"
4. Edit by voice: "delete that," "select all"

Accessibility typing features:

1. Settings > Accessibility > Interaction and dexterity
2. Useful options:
    - **Sticky keys**: Hold modifier keys without continuous pressure
    - **Slow keys**: Delay before key presses register
    - **Bounce keys**: Ignore rapid repeated presses

Lock Screen and Security Customization

Lock screen information display:

1. Settings > Lock screen > Widgets
2. Available widgets:
   - **Weather**: Current conditions and forecast
   - **Calendar**: Upcoming appointments
   - **Music**: Playback controls
   - **Digital wellbeing**: Usage statistics

Lock screen shortcuts:

1. Settings > Lock screen > Shortcuts
2. Customize bottom corner icons:
   - **Camera**: Quick photo access
   - **Flashlight**: Emergency lighting
   - **Voice recorder**: Quick memos
   - **Any frequently used app**

Security method selection: Pattern lock:

- Pros: Quick, visual, one-handed operation
- Cons: Visible smudges on screen, shoulder surfing

PIN lock:

- Pros: Familiar, works with gloves
- Cons: Can be observed, slower entry

Password lock:

- Pros: Most secure, complex combinations
- Cons: Slower entry, easy to forget

Biometric security:

- Fingerprint: Fast, secure, works in most conditions
- Face recognition: Convenient but less secure, lighting dependent

Lock screen timeout settings:

1. Settings > Lock screen > Secure lock settings
2. "Lock automatically after": 5 seconds to 30 minutes
3. Balance security vs convenience
4. Shorter timeouts for public use, longer for home

Lock screen notifications:

1. Settings > Lock screen > Notifications
2. Options:
    - **Show content**: Full message preview
    - **Hide content**: Show sender only
    - **Don't show**: No lock screen notifications

Making Your A16 5G Truly Yours

Creating efficient home screen layout:

1. Group related apps in folders:
   - **Communication**: Phone, Messages, Email
   - **Health**: Samsung Health, medication apps, doctor contacts
   - **Entertainment**: Music, photos, games
   - **Utilities**: Calculator, flashlight, weather

Widget strategy for seniors:

- **Clock widget**: Large, easy-to-read time display
- **Weather widget**: Daily conditions without opening app
- **Calendar widget**: Upcoming appointments at glance
- **Contacts widget**: One-tap calling for important people

Edge panel customization:

1. Settings > Display > Edge panels
2. Useful panels:
   - **Apps edge**: Frequently used apps
   - **People edge**: Important contacts
   - **Tools edge**: Flashlight, timer, calculator

Bixby Routines for personalization: Morning routine:

- Trigger: 7:00 AM weekdays
- Actions: Turn off Do Not Disturb, read calendar, open weather

Bedtime routine:

- Trigger: 9:00 PM
- Actions: Enable Do Not Disturb, dim screen, set morning alarm

Driving routine:

- Trigger: Connect to car Bluetooth
- Actions: Open navigation, enable hands-free mode, read messages aloud

Accessibility shortcuts:

1. Settings > Accessibility > Advanced settings > Accessibility shortcuts
2. Assign useful features to:
    - **Volume buttons**: Magnification, high contrast
    - **Side button**: Voice assistant, emergency calls
    - **Triple-tap screen**: Magnifier, color inversion

Personal emergency information:

1. Settings > Safety and emergency > Medical info
2. Add critical information accessible from lock screen:
    - Medical conditions
    - Allergies
    - Current medications
    - Emergency contact numbers
    - Blood type

Final personalization checklist:

- [ ] Set ringtone you'll recognize in noisy environments
- [ ] Configure lock screen with essential information
- [ ] Organize home screen with most-used apps
- [ ] Set up emergency contacts and medical information
- [ ] Create helpful routines for daily activities
- [ ] Adjust text size and display settings for comfort
- [ ] Test accessibility features that might help
- [ ] Backup personalization settings to Samsung Cloud

Your A16 5G should feel like a natural extension of your daily routine, not a complicated device you struggle to use. Take time to experiment with these settings – you can always revert changes if they don't improve your experience.

CHAPTER 11: FUTURE-PROOFING AND LONG-TERM OWNERSHIP

Your Galaxy A16 5G represents a significant investment that should serve you well for several years. Understanding Samsung's support timeline, making smart accessory choices, and properly maintaining your device ensures you get maximum value from your purchase. Unlike the rapid upgrade cycles that dominated early smartphone years, modern devices like the A16 5G offer genuine longevity when properly managed.

This final chapter helps you make informed decisions about long-term ownership, from recognizing when upgrades make sense to protecting your investment's resale value. You'll learn to distinguish between necessary accessories and marketing gimmicks, and understand how to prepare for an eventual transition to your next device.

Software Support Timeline and Update Strategy

Samsung's A16 5G support commitment:

- Security updates: 5 years (until 2029)
- Major Android updates: 4 years (through Android 18)

- One UI updates: Regular feature improvements throughout support period

Update categories and timing: Security patches (monthly):

- Install immediately when available
- Small downloads (50-200MB)
- Critical for protection against new threats
- No significant interface changes

Quarterly feature updates:

- New Samsung features and improvements
- Interface refinements and bug fixes
- Safe to install after 1-2 weeks
- May require settings readjustment

Annual Android updates:

- Major version upgrades (Android 15, 16, etc.)
- Significant interface changes possible
- Wait 2-4 weeks for stability reports
- Back up device before installing

Update strategy for seniors:

1. Enable automatic security updates
2. Manual approval for major updates
3. Read update notes before installing
4. Update during low-usage periods
5. Ensure 3GB+ free storage before updates

Accessory Ecosystem: What's Worth Buying
Essential accessories:

Screen protection:

- Tempered glass protector: $15-25
- Installation service: $10-15 (recommended)
- Replace when cracked or lifting

Case protection:

- **Basic protection**: Silicone case with raised edges ($15-30)
- **Enhanced protection**: OtterBox Defender-style ($40-60)
- **Senior-friendly**: Cases with wrist straps or belt clips

Charging accessories:

- Samsung 25W fast charger: $25
- Car charger with USB-C: $20-30
- Wireless charging pad: $30-50 (convenience vs. speed trade-off)
- Portable battery pack: $25-40 for emergencies

Audio accessories:

- Wired USB-C headphones: $20-50 (no battery concerns)
- Bluetooth earbuds: Samsung Galaxy Buds series ($100-200)
- Bluetooth speaker: For home use ($50-150)

Accessories to avoid:

- Cheap cables from unknown brands (fire risk)
- "Signal boosters" or "antenna enhancers" (ineffective)
- Screen cleaning "kits" (microfiber cloth sufficient)
- Phone "coolers" or "performance enhancers"

Smart home integration:

- Samsung SmartThings hub: Controls compatible devices
- Smart plugs: Remote appliance control
- Smart lights: Voice/app controlled lighting
- Smart door locks: Enhanced security with phone integration

When to Upgrade vs When to Stick with Your A16 5G

Signs it's time to upgrade:

- Battery lasts less than half a day with normal use
- Phone frequently freezes or crashes after troubleshooting
- Storage constantly full despite cleanup efforts
- Camera quality significantly inferior to current needs
- Essential apps no longer supported
- Physical damage affecting daily use

Reasons to keep your A16 5G:

- Still receiving security updates
- Performance meets daily needs
- Camera quality satisfactory for your use
- Storage adequate with cloud services
- All needed apps function properly
- Device physically sound

Upgrade timing considerations: Optimal upgrade windows:

- Years 3-4 for normal users
- Year 5+ for light users
- Immediately if device damaged beyond repair
- When carrier offers significant trade-in value

Poor upgrade timing:

- First 2 years (minimal improvements justify cost)
- During financial stress
- When current device meets all needs
- Immediately after major Android update (wait for stability)

Future-proofing your current device:

1. Maintain 15% free storage minimum
2. Install security updates promptly
3. Use cloud storage for photos/videos
4. Clean cache and optimize monthly
5. Physical protection with quality case

Resale Value Protection and Device Care

Maintaining resale value: Physical condition:

- Screen protector from day one
- Quality case always in use
- Regular cleaning with appropriate materials
- Avoid smoking around device
- Store in cool, dry locations

Software maintenance:

- Keep software updated
- Factory reset before selling
- Maintain original packaging and accessories
- Document any repairs with receipts

Resale value timeline:

- Year 1: 60-70% of original price
- Year 2: 40-50% of original price
- Year 3: 25-35% of original price
- Year 4+: 15-25% of original price

Where to sell for best value:

1. **Samsung trade-in program**: Convenient, guaranteed acceptance
2. **Carrier trade-ins**: Good value with new device purchase
3. **Swappa**: Dedicated phone marketplace, fair pricing
4. **eBay**: Largest audience, more work required

5. **Local classifieds**: Quick cash, meet-in-person risks

Pre-sale preparation:

1. Back up important data
2. Sign out of all accounts
3. Factory reset device
4. Clean physical condition
5. Include original accessories
6. Take clear photos for listings

Preparing for Your Next Samsung Galaxy Device

Data migration planning:

- Maintain Samsung Cloud backups
- Organize photos in albums
- Document important app settings
- List essential apps for quick reinstallation
- Note customization preferences

Learning curve minimization: Stick with Samsung ecosystem:

- Similar interface across Galaxy devices
- Settings transfer automatically
- Accessories often compatible
- Familiar troubleshooting procedures

Future device considerations:

- Similar or larger screen size for familiarity
- Improved camera systems for better photos
- Longer battery life for extended use
- Enhanced durability for active lifestyles

Timing your next purchase: Best buying periods:

- September-October: New model releases, previous year discounts
- Black Friday/Cyber Monday: Significant carrier deals
- Spring: Carrier promotional periods
- End of month/quarter: Sales quota pushes

Technology trends affecting seniors:

- **Larger screens**: Easier reading and interaction
- **Better cameras**: Clearer photos of grandchildren
- **Longer battery life**: Reduced charging anxiety
- **Enhanced accessibility**: Improved vision/hearing assistance
- **Simpler interfaces**: Less confusing navigation

Preparation timeline: 6 months before upgrade:

- Research new models and features
- Monitor pricing trends
- Evaluate current device performance
- Plan budget for new device and accessories

1 month before upgrade:

- Compare carrier deals and promotions
- Verify trade-in values
- Update current device for best trade-in condition
- Complete data backup verification

Upgrade day:

- Transfer data using Smart Switch
- Test all essential functions
- Set up security features immediately
- Gradually install apps rather than all at once

Your Galaxy A16 5G should provide 3-5 years of reliable service with proper care. When the time comes to upgrade, your experience with this device will make the transition to newer Samsung technology much smoother.

CONCLUSION

Your journey with the Samsung Galaxy A16 5G doesn't end with reading this guide – it begins here. Throughout these pages, we've explored every aspect of your device, from the excitement of unboxing to the practical realities of long-term ownership. The Galaxy A16 5G represents Samsung's understanding that seniors want capable technology without unnecessary complexity, and with the knowledge you've gained, you're equipped to unlock its full potential.

The most important lesson from this comprehensive guide is that you don't need to master everything at once. Start with the basics – making calls, sending messages, taking photos – then gradually incorporate the advanced features that genuinely improve your daily life. Your phone should adapt to your needs, not the other way around. Whether you're using it to stay connected with family, capture precious memories, or maintain your independence through helpful apps and features, the A16 5G has the capability to enhance rather than complicate your life.

Remember that technology is simply a tool, and like any tool, its value comes from how well it serves your specific needs. Some features we've discussed will become daily essentials, while others may never interest you – and that's perfectly fine. The customization options we've explored ensure your phone works exactly the way you want it to work. From adjusting text size for easier reading to setting up emergency features for peace of mind, every modification should make your device more useful and comfortable for your unique situation.

As you continue using your Galaxy A16 5G, don't hesitate to revisit specific chapters when you need guidance. Technology confidence builds gradually through practice and experience. The accessibility features, automation tools, and organizational strategies we've covered will become more valuable as you discover how they fit into your routine. Your phone will evolve alongside your comfort level, revealing new possibilities as you become more familiar with its capabilities.

Looking ahead, the A16 5G will serve you well for years to come with proper care and maintenance. Samsung's commitment to long-term software support means your device will remain secure and functional well into the future. When the time eventually comes to consider your next smartphone, the skills and preferences you've developed with the A16 5G will make that transition smooth and informed.

Technology should empower, not intimidate. With your Galaxy A16 5G as a reliable companion and this guide as your reference, you're prepared to embrace the conveniences of modern smartphone technology while maintaining control over your digital experience. Your phone is now truly yours – configured, customized, and ready to enhance your daily life in meaningful ways.

Welcome to confident smartphone ownership. Your Galaxy A16 5G adventure starts now.

www.ingramcontent.com/pod-product-compliance
Lightning Source LLC
LaVergne TN
LVHW060158190925
821494LV00009B/278